THE POWER OF DHARMA

THE UNIVERSAL MORAL PRINCIPLE

DR. NICHOLAS SUTTON

HANUMAN DASS

JAICO PUBLISHING HOUSE

Ahmedabad Bangalore Bhopal Bhubaneswar Chennai
Delhi Hyderabad Kolkata Lucknow Mumbai

Published by Jaico Publishing House
A-2 Jash Chambers, 7-A Sir Phirozshah Mehta Road
Fort, Mumbai - 400 001
jaicopub@jaicobooks.com
www.jaicobooks.com

THE POWER OF DHARMA
ISBN 978-81-8495-833-1

Jaico Impression: 2016

Printed by
Snehesh Printers
320-A, Shah & Nahar Ind. Est. A-1
Lower Parel, Mumbai - 400 013

"*The Power of Dharma is a gracious gift to the world. This book represents the true spirit of India but in addition it also shows the relevance of the ancient wisdom to modern times. The Power of Dharma is a bridge between past and present, between the East and the West and between the ancient and the modern.*"

Satish Kumar
Editor-in-Chief, Resurgence & Ecologist

The birth of poetry through compassion

After Valmiki, the illustrious sage, had learned all about the life of Lord Rama, he went to the river to bathe. Close to the river were two large and beautiful birds sweetly singing and playing together. A vicious hunter, who was plotting evil, shot an arrow which struck the male bird. Upon seeing her partner trembling on the ground, his body covered in blood, the hen cried out in great distress and in fear for her beloved's life. As Valmiki witnessed this ruthless hunter strike down the male bird, he became sad and thought to himself, 'This was not dharma, to kill a sweetly singing bird for no reason at all.' As he listened to the female hen pour her heart out he said to the hunter, 'After what you have done to this bird, peace will be no more than a word.' Then Valmiki realised that he had unintentionally created a work of poetry and he named the metre 'shloka' because it was spoken in 'shoka' (sadness). And thus it was due to a writer's overwhelming compassion for other living beings that poetry was born in India.

About the Authors

Dr Nicholas Sutton is Director of Continuing Education at the Oxford Centre for Hindu Studies. He obtained his BA Degree with First Class Honours from the Department of Theology at the University of Birmingham in 1991 and gained his Phd from Lancaster University in 1995, submitting a doctoral thesis on the religious teachings of the Mahabharata.

Hanuman Dass is Founder of GoDharmic.com a platform for social change with over 96,000 users. Inspired by Hinduism he works closely with a wide range of organisations to promote a better understanding of Indian philosophy and its practical application in the modern world. He is a long time student of ex-Harvard Professor Ram Dass (Richard Alpert) and is also Managing Director of Arjun Capital.

Contents

1

Introduction

The world is now an interconnected global village and there are many reasons for us all to be optimistic. There have been significant advances in medicine which have eradicated deadly diseases; millions have been lifted from poverty by powerful initiatives such as micro-lending; the works of philanthropic organisations and modern education have improved the lives of millions of young people. Slavery in most parts of the world has become unthinkable and hopefully something we can end forever.

Perhaps more than at any time in recent history we are awakening to the fact that the wellbeing of our own bodies and that of the environment requires particular care and attention. The internet has in many ways helped to break down artificial boundaries between people around the world enabling communication, trade, and common understanding at a deeper and faster rate than ever before. Discrimination against people for their gender, race, religion, or sexual persuasion is also looked down upon in most parts of the modern world.

However, despite these positive advances we still face tremendous challenges ahead. We live in a heavily populated world of over 7 billion people with 1.3 billion living off less than $1.25 per day. The stark reality is that every 24 hours there are approximately 220,000 more mouths to feed than the previous day whilst the availability of food and water is declining. The gap between the haves and the have-nots grows ever wider. Even in the USA, an extremely prosperous nation, the wealth gap shows that the top 1% possesses a greater collective wealth than the bottom 90 %. We can only imagine how large the difference is when compared to the poor of the developing world who cannot even meet the most basic requirements of food and uncontaminated water.

Power struggles, armed conflict and threats from weapons of mass destruction still plague our world; Palestine, Syria, Sri Lanka, Afghanistan, and Iraq are places where millions of children will grow up in fear on a day to day basis. Drones now systematically take undervalued lives as if in some nightmarish computer game. Pakistan, a country with 185 million people tightly packed into an area only 8% the size of the United States, has lost 90% of its original forests and spends a staggering 44 times more on its military budget than on health and family planning, a trend that is similar in India and many other countries.

The environment is becoming an increasing concern to everybody's life. Extreme climatic conditions and natural disasters are making agriculture, soil conservation, and reforestation problematic. C,ontamination of land and sea is causing the deterioration of animal and plant life faster than any time in recorded history, whilst global warming and our insatiable appetite for burning fossil fuels is ever increasing as the developing countries follow the development models of the prosperous nations.

So what can we do about all of this?

It is certainly a possibility that we cannot change anything at all. So should we just focus on our own personal lives and leave everyone else to do the same? Of course there is no simple stop gap solution for these issues, but we do believe that for change to occur there has to be a fundamental shift towards a greater emphasis on virtue and right action. At every level of society, be it government, business, religion or the individual, what is required is a shift in priority from a material preoccupation towards a more ethical approach to life, where we act out of a sense of responsibility and for the benefit of all beings.

One may ask whether there can be any genuine moral standards in our complex world. With the help of ancient Indian texts we hope to encourage and stimulate a thought-provoking exploration into the nature of right action and the inner values we believe are so crucial for overcoming the disconnectedness and displaced priorities that currently pervade our approaches to life. But how is it possible to use Indian or Hindu writings when there remain so much inequality, corruption, poverty, and caste discrimination in India today, along with a patriarchal social system where women are treated as second class citizens?

Here the point to be made is that the highest thought will always transcend its context, and hence we should consider the values and insights presented here on their own terms. When they are read in this way, without necessarily applying the label of Hindu or even Indian, we begin to see that these ideals, espoused form an excellent platform, counter every form of discriminatory practice, including those that have blighted the culture of India over many centuries. Accepting the consideration that there will undoubtedly be proclamations in ancient texts that will go against our current ethical standards, we attempt to present the profound eternal law of dharma.

The majority of the narratives used in this book are derived from the Mahabharata, the world's longest poem, a monumental Hindu text which at its core reveals the subtle art of dharma, the law of morality and right action. It is roughly ten times the length of the Iliad and Odyssey combined and fifteen times the size of the Bible. Yet it is so much more than a linear narrative; in many ways it explores, rather than dictates ethical action. The Mahabharata is an encyclopaedia of spiritual and moral insights as well as a multi-dimensional repository of ideas on personal, political and psychological action.

One of the key personalities in the epic is Duryodhana, who is characterised as inherently immoral, deceitful and always pursuing his own narrow self-interest. He is never gentle in his words, thoughts or deeds, and his philosophy is sometimes frighteningly similar to the "'greed is good'" mentality. He insists that "'dissatisfaction with one's lot, however great, is a positive quality, for such a state of mind is the root of success'". Duryodhana's views can be startlingly similar to those shared in today's competitive business environments. He persistently seeks competition and conflict, entirely disregarding all moral restraints. By contrast, his cousin Yudhishthira is righteousness personified; he "'weeps with all living beings'", and constantly asserts that non-violence and universal compassion are the great features of dharma. Although an in-depth analysis of this profound epic and the other works we have made use of is beyond the scope of this project, it is hoped that the powerful narratives, which have had a substantial effect on South Asia for thousands of years, can provide a breath of fresh air, enriching and adding value to our modern predicaments by highlighting the petty-mindedness and materialistic greed which can so easily overtake us.

For humanity to collectively confront the sufferings of the world, we will need a change towards an increased commitment to real virtue or *daya bhuteshu* ("'compassion for all living beings'"). Kindness, non-violence, and generosity are the flags for this philosophy. Most of us recognise these positive attributes but too often we get distracted by the minutiae of daily life. It is with this aim in mind that we write this book and run Godharmic.com as our platform for positive social action, working with various charities, businesses, and Government bodies to try to help alleviate suffering in small but significant ways. Our first two campaigns are to promote organic farming as a dharmic choice, and to raise awareness and funding for the education and housing of underprivileged girls in the developing world. These are just two of the thousands of causes that could be taken up as a means of actualising the philosophy of dharma.

Our aim is to present ancient passages which inspire a move towards kindness and compassion, making us realise what is truly great about humanity and our relationship with the world, urging us to go beyond our baser impulses and love our neighbour, and finaly not to blindly follow dogma but to think carefully about all of the various choices in life and act as we see fit.

With Love,
Hanuman Dass

2

What is Dharma?

*The scriptures are different from one another; there is not a
single saint whose opinion can be accepted by everyone; the
truth about dharma and duty is hidden in the cave of our
heart: therefore, that alone is the path along which the great
have trod.*
Yudhisthira, Yaksha-prashna, Vana-parvan, Mahabharata

*Two things awe me most, the starry sky above me and the
moral law within me.*
Immanuel Kant

In early Indian philosophy, the word "'dharma'" is used to
indicate the defining characteristic of an object, the quality
that makes it what it is. In that sense the power to radiate
light and heat could be said to be the dharma of fire. And
when applied to humanity, dharma really means the same
thing—it is that quality that epitomises what it is to be truly
human. In this light the view of human nature is extremely
optimistic as we hope this discussion will demonstrate.

As the use of the word dharma developed in Indian
thought, it increasingly came to be applied to human conduct and in particular to indicate the form of ethical lifestyle
that represented the ideal for humanity to strive towards. Of
course, there will always be debates over what constitutes
the ideal way of living, and we will consider some of these
later on, but essentially dharma means to live in harmony
with the world in a manner that is virtuous and compassionate, seeking the welfare of all rather than one's own nar-

row self-interest.

So whilst it is natural to presume that the concept of dharma and the very use of the word itself indicate some connection with Hindu or Buddhist teachings, the concept of dharma transcends all boundaries of race and creed and reflects universal human values. What we understand as dharma will be equally relevant to people of all religions and to those who have no interest in religion at all. The idea of dharma does certainly occur frequently in Hindu texts whilst the Buddha referred to his teachings as "'the Dhamma'" ("'dharma'" in the Pali language), and we will be making use of material from these Indian sources. Although we are Hindus, it should be emphasised that there is no intention to proselytise on behalf of any particular religious tradition; what we are doing is using Indian resources to prompt discussion of global humanitarian values. From our perspective, whether one is a Christian, Jew, Hindu, Muslim, Sikh or Buddhist (or regards all religion as ridiculous) is of no concern. We hope it will become abundantly clear that the understanding of dharma we are trying to convey goes far beyond any narrow designation and can embrace the ideals of believers and non-believers alike.

With these preliminaries in place, we can now proceed to consider more precisely what we might mean by dharma. It was previously implied that to adhere to dharma meant to move away from mere self-interest and to consider one's actions in relation to the welfare of all living beings. But how can this be achieved? There are a number of issues to be considered. Dharma could be regarded as one's duty towards family members or to society as a whole, ensuring that the responsibilities related to one's position in life are fully accepted, regardless of how onerous or challenging they may become. On the other hand, dharma could be understood in a more abstract sense as pure virtue and the consistent application of virtue to each new situation that arises. Alternatively, we might try to codify dharma and draw up an extensive list of "dos" and "don'ts" through which conduct can be regulated; this of course is an approach typically adopted by world religions as with the Jewish law, the Hindu dharma-shastra or the Islamic Shariah.

All of these are possible ways of instituting and practising the dharmic approach to life, but it is probably better to think of dharma as the ideal state of mind that brings one closest to the full manifestation of humanity. Dharma hence means a state of consciousness by which compassion and good will towards all beings is instinctive, and the practical application of that mentality is enacted without ordinance or stricture. For an idea to be meaningful it must lead to a tangible manifestation—in relation to dharma that means action to promote the welfare of the world. The point here is that a person who cultivates the dharmic state of mind will instinctively manifest that state of consciousness in the form of specific acts of virtue that are beneficial for others in need.

But dharma is not just for saints who devote themselves entirely to philanthropic work; dharma is an ideal we work towards in our everyday lives. It is unlikely that we will ever encounter anyone who is entirely dharmic or indeed anyone in whom there is no trace of dharma. The point is that one should try to make small changes and move gradually but profoundly towards dharma.

At times the contemporary world can seem a depressing place beset by an ethos of individualism, competition and acquisition. The result is that whilst many, many people are condemned to lives of abject poverty, others can enjoy life-styles of unbelievable luxury. From the standpoint of justice and the standpoint of dharma this is unacceptable. We might blame the economic system or we might point to the ethos of the age, which raises acquisition above fairness and honesty, but, above all, this seems due to a loss of respect for the concept we are referring to as dharma. We are not expecting the world to change overnight or the rich to suddenly give away all their money, but what we do feel is that the promotion of the concept of dharma, and the advocacy of practical measures reflecting that state of consciousness might go some way towards making a difference. One might wish for a revolution that would change the very nature of the modern world, but from a more practical perspective we must be aware that even a small change that affects a single life is of profound and lasting significance. Any slight change of heart, any small act of kindness, is a turn towards dharma and is exactly what we mean by the request to 'go dharmic'.

3

East and West, Right and Wrong

Dharma is subtle.
Krishna, Mahabharata

*We have in fact, two kinds of morality, side by side: one that
we preach, but do not practice, and another that we practice,
but seldom preach.*
Bertrand Russell

One of the issues referred to earlier was the problem involved in determining what is right and what is wrong. Are there clear criteria on which to base any such conclusions? Probably not, and hence we frequently encounter the assertion that dharma is a subtle matter, which can be difficult to define precisely in relation to specific issues and circumstances. What we can be sure of, however, is that if we are successful in cultivating dharma as a state of mind, and in that way reaching closer to the fulfilment of our humanity, then we will certainly make more right decisions than wrong ones.

For example, in the teachings of the Jains (one of the religious groups in India) it is argued that what is right and what is wrong can be determined by applying the principle of *ahimsa* (literally, "'not harming'"). If an action supports that principle then it is right action and if it is not in accordance with ahimsa then it is deemed to be wrong. The problem then arises, however, as to how to determine whether or not a particular course of action will produce an outcome that promotes or contradicts the fundamental precept of not harming. Moreover, one must consider whether ahimsa is merely avoiding what is harmful, or whether it also implies positive action to undo the harm that others have wrought.

Whatever basis for moral action one adopts, there will be similar problems that each individual will have to try to resolve, and in doing so the main requirement is absolute honesty and being true to oneself. In the West, ethical discourse has often tended to take an absolutist turn with types of action being designated as either right or wrong and people being expected to adhere perfectly to what is right. For example, if a person has a belief in the morality of vegetarianism then the expectation is that he or she will adhere strictly to a vegetarian diet to the point of avoiding any food product that might contain the slightest trace of anything derived from a slaughtered animal. If the avowed vegetarian is found to be guilty of occasional lapses or deviations from that standard, he or she will likely to be labelled as a hypocrite.

This is a relatively clear-cut example but what about the dilemma over poverty? Most relatively affluent people will spend a portion of their money on luxury items such as holidays or entertainments that are not truly essential but which bring them a certain amount of pleasure. Every time we spend money on these non-essential items we are making a choice. A lot of us could spend our £10 to help provide a home for an abandoned child or to maintain the sight of a person who is going blind; alternatively, we could spend it on what is essentially a selfish pleasure. From a moral perspective we may know exactly what we should do with our £10 but we are equally aware that we are not going to make that right choice in every case. Are we then hypocrites? Not really, we are just people who are not able to live up to the standard of morality we believe in.

The response to this problem may lie with a form of ethics that accepts partial or gradual adherence to moral precepts and does not demand absolutism in their implementation. Very few of us are saints or bodhisattvas but that does not mean we should therefore simply give up, or indeed try to invent a false morality that justifies our own shortcomings. Rather we need to accept that even though absolute perfection is unlikely, to do something, however small, is always better than to do nothing at all. To go back to our original example, one may believe that vegetarianism is morally right but finds that to live absolutely by that precept is beyond one's present powers. In such a case a person might try to be vegetarian for just one day a week as with the Meatless Monday campaign or simply as much as possible. There is no hypocrisy there, simply the acceptance that whilst we may fall short of perfection we can all do a little more than we did previously. This idea of gradual or partial implementation of moral standards is very typical of the Indian approach and is overwhelmingly healthy.

Somewhere along the line western culture has become obsessed with the idea of guilt and absolute standards in a way that is wholly unrealistic. Guilt is such a negative emotion that it will rarely lead to anything worthwhile. A person suffering from the imposition of guilt is unlikely to do anything differently because the progress it is possible for that person to make will still be deemed inadequate. What tends to happen instead is that we devise false values designed primarily to justify our own conduct. Hence the advice must always be to be wary of any statement of principle that coincides with one's own self-interest; it will usually have been created for the purpose of justification rather than providing an impulse towards right action.

Let us be gentle with ourselves and with others as well, for condemnation and calumny will rarely lead to anything positive. We can establish absolute standards but we can also accept that in all likelihood we will not live up to them in every situation. The positive aspect is that every so often we will forego the luxury and donate our £10 or our time to something that is more in accordance with dharma; and then perhaps the next time it will be a little more or a little more often. The ideal behind promoting dharma is gentle rather than harsh; it encourages all positive actions, however great or small, and is inclined to celebrate achievement rather than to condemn failure.

4

The Nachiketas Way

In life both the sreyas (the good) and the preyas (the pleasur-able) will approach a person. One who is wise will consider them carefully, note the distinction between them, and then opt for the sreyas over the preyas. The fool, however, seeks the acquisition and preservation of material objects and hence selects the preyas.
Mrityu, 2.2, Katha Upanishad

It is our choices, Harry, that show us what we truly are, far more than our abilities.
J.K. Rowling, Harry Potter and the Chamber of Secrets

The Katha Upanishad is one of the major Upanishads that form the philosophical portion of the Vedas. Nobody knows for certain when the Katha Upanishad was composed. Indi-an sources have traditionally argued for a date of remote an-tiquity but most modern scholars would suggest sometime around 300 or 200 BC. The main theme of this Upanishad is the possibility of life after death and the existence of a soul or *atman*, but for the purposes of our consideration of dharma and right action we should focus on the first couple of chap-ters, which provide a setting for the full discussion. Here we encounter Nachiketas, a young boy who is cast out by his angry father and sent to be with Death who here takes on a personified form as Mrityu, the deity who takes life away. Because he is made to wait at the door of Mrityu's house he is offered three boons in recompense and for the third of these he asks to know the secret of whether or not existence continues after death. It is at this point that we take up the discussion.

From the Katha Upanishad, Chapter One

20. Nachiketas: This doubt arises over a person who has died, for some say, 'He still exists'" whilst others say, "'He no longer exists'. I want you to instruct me so that I can understand this point; this is the third of my wishes.

21. Mrityu: Even the gods of ancient times were uncertain about this, for the essence of the matter is subtle and hence difficult to comprehend. So please select a different boon to ask of me, Nachiketas; do not insist on this request; release me from it.

22. Nachiketas: So even the gods are uncertain on this point and you say it is hard to comprehend. But I will not find anyone like you to explain it and there is no gift you can give that will equal the one I have requested.

23. Mrityu: Choose sons and grandsons who will live for a hundred years or vast herds of animals, elephants, gold or horses. Choose an expansive region of the earth where you can live for as many years as you wish.

24. If you consider it to be a blessing of equal worth then choose both wealth and long life. You may rise to a position of power throughout the vast earth and I will ensure that you enjoy all the objects of desire.

25. There are so many desirable things unobtainable in this mortal world but now you may ask for anything you wish for. Look, here are beautiful women with chariots

and musical instruments; such as these are never acquired by men of this world. You can be served by these
women, now they are offered by me, Nachiketas, but do
not inquire further about the subject of death.

26. Nachiketas: For a mortal being, O Death, the passing
of time takes away the vigour of all the senses and even
the full duration of life is just a moment. So let these car-
riages remain with you; let this dancing and singing stay
yours.

27. Wealth does not make any man content and anyway
I will certainly attain wealth now that I have seen you. I
will live only for as long as you ordain, so this alone is the
gift I ask for.

28. Having encountered the gods who neither age nor
die, what earth-bound man subject to old age and death
but possessing true understanding will take pleasure in a
long life when he considers the true nature of the beauty,
pleasure and delight that are to be gained here?

29. This is what people are uncertain about, Mrityu, what
happens at the time of the great transition. So this is what
you should tell me about. Apart from this wish, the entry
to a great mystery, there is nothing else that Nachiketas
asks for.

Katha Upanishad, Chapter Two

1. Mrityu: The good (*sreyas*) is one thing and the pleasing
(*preyas*) is something different. Their ends are different
but both bind a man. Good comes to one who accepts

the *sreyas* but one who chooses the *preyas* fails to achieve his purpose.

2. In life both the *sreyas* and the *preyas* will approach a person. One who is wise will consider them carefully, note the distinction between them, and then opt for the *sreyas* over the *preyas*. The fool, however, seeks the acquisition and preservation of material objects and hence selects the *preyas*.

3. You, Nachiketas, have considered these objects of desire, so delightful with their pleasing forms, and have then rejected them. You have not sought the path that abounds in wealth because of which so many people sink down.

4. That which is known as wisdom (*vidya*) and that which is known as ignorance (*avidya*) are entirely distinct and move in different directions. I now consider Nachiketas to be one who seeks wisdom because these multifarious objects of desire did not tempt you.

This preliminary discussion serves as an introduction to the discourse given by Mrityu to Nachiketas on the existence of the immortal soul, which is the principal theme of the Katha Upanishad. The subject matter thus introduced is esoteric and mystical but we can take the substance of what is said in the passage cited above and apply it to our consideration of dharma. After Mrityu has offered his temptations to Nachiketas, he points out at the start of Chapter 2 that throughout life all people face the type of choices he defines with the words *sreyas* and *preyas*. *Sreyas* is the right thing to do whilst *preyas* is the option that leads to our own gratification.

If we apply this notion to the previous debate and to the central idea behind the option for dharma, we can see that so often in life we face exactly this choice between doing what is beneficial from a selfish perspective, the *preyas*, and trying to apply the principles of dharma, which would be the *sreyas*. In line with the ideas presented in our discussion of the ethical context, it is not to be expected that we will be able to opt for *sreyas* every time; that would be unrealistic. But the ethos behind 'Go Dharmic' is that as far as possible, and more often than we do now, we try to embrace the *sreyas*, forgoing the *preyas* which brings instant gratification in terms of wealth and pleasure; opting for what is right rather than what is instantly pleasing.

This may seem to be an overly simplistic way of looking at things but it is sometimes the case that the simplest assertions are also the most profound. Within the Indian traditions, Valmiki's great work, the Ramayana, tells of the life of Rama and his endeavours to overcome adversity. Many Hindus revere Rama as a Deity and regard the Ramayana as a devotional work but of greater significance is the emphasis Valmiki places on dharma and the way in which Rama always opts to act in accordance with dharma, however difficult his position may be. We may find the complex analysis of dharma contained within the Mahabharata more satisfying, but on the other hand the simplicity of its message can be seen as the great strength of Valmiki's work. Just as Mrityu draws a stark division between the *sreyas* and the *preyas*, so the Ramayana portrays the life of Rama in similarly unequivocal terms. At the beginning of the Ramayana, in its very first chapter, Valmiki describes Rama's nature to the sage Narada: "'He is wise and grounded in proper conduct'", and "'he knows the ways of righteousness and is always true to his word. The welfare of his citizens is his constant concern. He is renowned, learned, pure, disciplined, and contemplative.'" He goes on to explain how Rama is "'the protector of all living beings and the guardian of righteousness'", "'the ultimate resort for good men, as is the ocean for the rivers, and noble and equable in all circumstances and always a pleasure to behold'".

Rama faces a series of harsh choices but at all times he opts for what is right over what is gratifying, and it is this simple but profound message of the Ramayana that has resonated down the centuries since the time of its composition thousands of years ago.

5

Krishna's Common-sense Dharma

Anyone who adheres blindly to the principle of speaking the truth is no better than a fool.
Krishna, Mahabharata

I always tell the truth. Even when I lie.
Al Pacino in *Scarface*

The passage here is a loose translation of a section of the Mahabharata, which occurs in the latter stages of the final conflict at Kurukshetra. Arjuna is given the task of guarding his elder brother, Yudhishthira, but is forced to go to another part of the battlefield to confront a group of dangerous adversaries who are gaining the upper hand. Whilst Arjuna is elsewhere, Karna leads an attack on Yudhishthira in the course of which the latter is painfully wounded and forced to flee before the foe. He is suffering terrible pain because of his wounds as well as a sense of humiliation at having to turn his back on the enemy, and in this state of torment he addresses angry words at Arjuna, condemning his prowess and saying that he should give up his mighty bow, the Gandiva, and pass it on to a warrior better able to use it. These words of Yudhishthira are unjust to Arjuna, for he is speaking in a state of acute anguish, but the situation is made even worse when Arjuna reveals that he has vowed to behead anyone who says that he should give up the Gandiva bow. For Arjuna a vow can never be broken and so he draws his sword to strike down Yudhishthira. At this point Krishna intervenes:

Mahabharata, Book 8 (Karna-parvan), Chapter 49

Krishna then said to Arjuna, 'Stop! Stop! No one who understands the distinctions of dharma would ever act in such a way. You do not know about the decisions made by learned men who teach disciples about matters of right conduct. It is never easy to determine what course of action should be followed and what should be avoided, but it may be possible if one follows the guidance of scripture. You think that you know what dharma is, but by acting in this way as if it were dharma you are showing your ignorance of dharma, for the killing of a living being is forbidden by those who truly adhere to dharma. In my opinion, never killing any living being is the highest dharma; one may speak a falsehood but one should never kill another being. So how is it that you are prepared to kill the king, your elder brother, who is himself one who comprehends dharma? The vow you took was an act of folly and now as another act of folly you are preparing to embrace adharma [the opposite of dharma]. Why are you going to do this without thinking properly about dharma? The true end of dharma is certainly a subtle matter, which is hard to understand.

'"Now listen to a narration which reflects on the subtle and complex nature of dharma. One who speaks the truth adheres to dharma; there is no virtue higher than truthfulness. However, the practice of the essence of truth can be very difficult to comprehend. There are a number of occasions on which one may speak a lie: at a marriage, to woo a woman, when one's life or property is threatened and for the sake of a Brahmana. On such occasions falsehood becomes truth and truth becomes falsehood. Anyone who adheres blindly to the principle of speaking the truth is no better than a fool.

"'There was a holy man named Kausika who was not well read in the teachings on dharma. He lived at a good distance from any village, at a place where a number of rivers met, and he had taken the following vow: 'I must always speak the truth.' He became famous for his adherence to this principle. Once some people came to the forest where he lived, attempting to escape with their possessions from a gang of ferocious robbers. The robbers then approached Kausika and said, 'A host of people came by here a little while ago. Which way did they go?' Kausika told the truth, 'They entered this wood here.' Acting on this information, the robbers pursued their victims and when they found them they killed them all. And because of the adharma of speaking the truth, Kausika was reborn in a low state of life.

"'There has to be some way of distinguishing dharma. Some say the highest knowledge is gained through reason (*tarka*) but many others say one gains knowledge of dharma from the Shruti (scriptures). I do not disagree with this, but the Shruti does not refer to each individual case. Dharma was created for the welfare of living beings and hence whatever sustains living beings is dharma. So we must understand dharma as that which leads to the welfare of people in the world. Now that I have given you a clear definition of dharma you must decide whether Yudhishthira should be slaughtered!'"

Arjuna accepts Krishna's sound advice, but asks if there is some way of getting out of this dilemma without breaking his sworn word. Krishna then suggests that as an insult is often said to be equal to death he might "'kill'" his elder brother with insulting words, thereby escaping from an impossible predicament. Arjuna accepts this guidance and the problem is resolved.

There are a number of relevant points in this passage, some more significant than others. We might start by noticing the emphasis placed on not killing or not harming, which is a consistent feature of Hindu ethics and a point we will return to in other sections. Secondly, one might be a little shocked by the "'robust'" attitude that Krishna takes towards truth and falsehood, particularly where he states that it is acceptable to be untruthful at a wedding or in wooing a woman. He does not elaborate on the point but it seems that what he is referring to is the type of flattery and exaggeration that often takes place at a social gathering when one is meeting up with acquaintances or distant relatives. One might not like some of these people but it would be impolite, pointless and disruptive to express one's true feelings. And in wooing a woman a young man may tend to exaggerate his own achievements in order to create a good impression, which is not exactly honest but at the same is not entirely reprehensible, given the situation.

The real point being here, however, is the insistence that any definition of dharma should not be overly prescriptive. Reference is made to the rigid codes one sometimes encounters, with Krishna arguing that a degree of flexibility is required by which each new situation is assessed on its own merits. Hence the point is made that whilst being truthful is usually a virtue, there are times when it is better to deviate from this principle and not feel oneself forced to adhere to a rule of conduct which in that situation is clearly dysfunctional.

Moreover, we are given a very simple understanding of the true nature of dharma; it is whatever course of action brings good to living beings.* This means that there are no fixed rules of religion or morality as each situation must be taken as unique; the test of determining what is for the good of living beings must then be applied with honesty and intelligence. It is interesting to note that at the end of his speech, Krishna still leaves it up to Arjuna to decide what is right or wrong based on the general principle he has enunciated. There are good lessons to learn from this discussion, particularly in the indication that right and wrong cannot and should not be reduced to a simplistic code of "dos" and "don'ts". We have our intelligence and if we can sustain our integrity and our honesty then the emphasis is on using these attributes to properly understand each situation without prejudice and on that basis determine for ourselves the right course of action to follow.

*The actual Sanskrit words used are as follows: *yah syad dharana-samyuktah sa dharma iti niscayah* (8.49.50) Here the word syat means "'it may be'" and the implication is that dharma is not set but will vary from one situation to another. Still, however, we have the words *dharana-samyukta*, which mean "'bringing about the maintenance, the sustenance or the well-being of all living beings'", which serves as the fundamental precept on which dharma is based.

6

Savitri and Eternal Dharma

Showing no malice towards any living being through actions,
thoughts or words; showing kindness to all and giving in
charity. This is the eternal dharma, the sanatana-dharma, as
defined by the righteous.
Savitri, Mahabharata

Perhaps in return for conquest, arrogance and spoliation,
India will teach us the tolerance and gentleness of the mature
mind, the quiet content of the unacquisitive soul, the calm of
the understanding spirit, and a unifying, a pacifying love for
all living things.
William Durant (1885 -1981)

The story of Savitri and Satyavan is widely known throughout India and indeed the Western world as well where it was made into an opera by Gustav Holst. In most of the popular retellings, the focus is on Savitri as the devoted wife whose love for her husband and commitment to his welfare deliver him from the hands of death. Less well known, however, are the exact words spoken by Savitri in order to win the favour of Yama, the God of Death, as he is carrying away the spirit of Satyavan into the afterlife. What we want to do here is to give the story as it appears in Book 3 of the Mahabharata but with emphasis on her speeches on dharma, which are presented in a verse by verse fashion. These verses provide a fascinating insight into the ways in which eternal (*sanatana*) dharma can be understood.

Yudhisthira asked the saint Markandeya, "'O mighty one,

I am not bothered by the loss of the kingdom; I am not even bothered for my brothers losing the kingdom. What truly bothers me is that Draupadi the princess has to suffer in this terrible way. She has undeservingly suffered on numerous occasions. Have you ever heard of or seen any woman as pure and perfect as princess Draupadi?'

Markandeya responded, "'Yes, indeed I have. Listen while I tell you the tale about Savitri. Once upon a time there was a king in Madras, who was filled with virtue and was famous for his pious disposition; he always cared for the saints, was good-natured and always kept his word. He controlled his senses through yoga practise and always performed the religious ceremonies. He was very charitable and was regarded as the foremost giver of wealth, and he was loved throughout the land in both the cities and the villages. The name of this great king was Aswapati. He always focused on the welfare of all living beings; he was forgiving and constantly spoke the truth whilst restraining his senses to the highest degree.

"'As time passed, and the celibate king grew older, he became increasingly concerned that he was childless. He decided to hold a great fire sacrifice making ten thousand offerings into the fire in honour of the Goddess Savitri and only stopping to eat after six hours. The virtuous king continued his strict vows for eighteen long years when one day Savitri appeared in an embodied form from the fire. The Goddess said,: "I have been pleased with your devotion; your purity, self-restraint and performance of vows has been exceptional and deserves great admiration! O Aswapati, ask for whatsoever you desire, I will grant you one wish, however, by no means should you show any disregard for dharma in your request."

"'Aswapati said, "It is through my desire for dharma that I have conducted my life in this way. O Goddess, my wish is to have hundreds of sons worthy of representing my lineage, so if you are truly pleased with me, do grant me this one wish." The Goddess Savitri responded, "O King, I was already aware of your desire and have spoken to the Lord about your sons. Through the grace of the one that is self-created, you shall have a single daughter of great ability. I am glad to give you this message on behalf of the Lord." Having accepted the words of Savitri, the king worshipped her hoping that the child would come soon. He then returned to his city to continue his righteous reign and his eldest wife, the princess of Malava, became pregnant. When the time came, a beautiful lotus-eyed daughter was born, and after performing the prescribed birth ceremonies they named her Savitri. She was like a goddess herself, an attractive damsel and a golden vision of beauty. The people considered her to be divine and she amazed all who came into contact with her.

"'On one occasion, after taking a bath in the river, she performed her prayers and ceremonies, and after offering flowers to the Deity she took them with her to meet her father. Seeing the graceful princess standing with hands joined, the king became sad and spoke, "My dear daughter, the time has come for you to get married but due to your energy no man has even dared to ask for your hand! I think you should find your own husband, somebody who will be able to match your perfect qualities. Search for a man of your liking and inform me; be sure to deliberate on it carefully. Go and search for your husband but do not act in a way that would offend the gods." Bowing at her father's feet and taking the blessings of the saints, the maiden departed on a golden chariot into the forests, distributing wealth at every place she visited.

"'One day King Aswapati was conversing with the illustrious sage Narada in his royal court when Savitri returned. Narada asked Aswapati where she had been and the king replied, "She left to find a suitable partner for herself and has finally returned; let us hear from her about the husband she has found!" Savitri said, "Amongst the Salwa people, I found a very virtuous king named Dyumatsena, who was completely blind and had one son. A long time ago, an old enemy of this king was hiding in the city and took advantage of his blindness to seize the kingdom away from him. King Dyumatsena was exiled into the forest with his wife and newborn baby. Having accepted life in the forests, the king practised many great vows and peformed various religious austerities. His son, although born in the city, was raised up in a forest hermitage and it is this young man who has stolen my heart. He is the perfect choice to be my husband." The sage Narada said, "Savitri, you have unknowingly committed a grave error. You have accepted Satyavan, the son of Dyumatsena and there is no doubt that he possesses excellent qualities. His mother and father always speak the truth and it is for this reason that the priests named him Satyavan. As a child he loved horses, he took great pleasure in making horses out of clay and was constantly drawing pictures of them; for this reason he was also given the nickname Chitraswa." The king then asked Narada, "Is this prince Satyavan devoted to his parents? Is he filled with energy, intelligence, forgiveness and courage?" To this Narada replied, "Satyavan is comparable to the Sun in energy, in wisdom he is equivalent to the creator himself, he is brave like Indra, lord of the heavens, and as forgiving as the Earth herself."

"'Aswapati then asked, "Is this prince liberal and always

giving, devoted to the priests, good looking, handsome? Please tell me more about him." Narada said, "He is the ultimate giver of gifts, famous for his truthfulness and he is beautiful like the moon. His senses are under complete control. He is meek, brave and truthful all at the same time! He shows great generosity to his friends, his character is flawless, and his conduct is always virtuous." Aswapati said, "So, you say he possesses every virtue? Is there anything wrong with this man?" Narada replied, "There is only one concern and that will cast a cloud over all the great things about him. In a year's time Satyavan will unfortunately pass away, his days are limited."

"'The king then said to his daughter, "My beautiful child, please reconsider and find another match, for this loss would be unbearable." Savitri said, "Whether his life is short or long, whether he has virtues or none, I have selected him as my husband and will stand firm by him." Narada said, "Your daughter's heart is with him and it is not possible to make her swerve from her path of virtue. Satyavan is a very honourable man and so I must give my blessings for this marriage." The king said, "Your words, Narada, should never be disobeyed for you are my guru." Narada replied, "Very well, let this marriage be attended by peace! It is time for me to depart, bless you all."

"'The king began to make the wedding arrangements and left for the hermitage to meet with Dyumsatsena in the sacred forest. When he arrived he saw the blind king seated on *kusha* grass under a great tree. After respectfully greeting him and introducing himself, the blind king asked Aswapati, "Why have you come here?"' Aswapati replied, "'This is my daughter Savitri who is blessed with beauty and morality, and I would like her to marry your son." Dyumatsena said,

"Having been deprived of the kingdom we are now living in the woods, so how will your daughter bear this hardship and difficult lifestyle?" Aswapati said, "My daughter and I both know that happiness and sadness come and go, neither is ever fixed, so there is no need for apprehension. I have come here with my mind made up, so please accept my daughter as a wife for Satyavan and let us join as equals."

"'With the blessings of both fathers, the marriage of Satyavan and Savitri then took place with great splendour. The newlyweds were overjoyed and were the perfect match, pleasing all members of their families. Savitri was an ideal wife, she spoke words as sweet as honey and was skilled in many tasks. She was in complete control of her temper. Filled with love they lived happily for many months but at the back of her mind Savitri always remembered Narada's words. She knew the time was fast approaching for her husband to depart this life, and despite the displeasure of her father decided to fast for three days for Satyavan's well being. When the fateful time came close, Savitri knew that the next day was destined to be his last and was deeply distressed. As she completed her three day fast she was persuaded by her father-in-law to take food. Satyavan lifted his axe upon his shoulders and prepared to leave the ashram to gather wood for the sacred fire they constantly maintained. Savitri said, "I am coming with you! I cannot bear to be separated from you!" Satyavan said, "You have never entered the forest before, and already you are weak from the difficult fast you undertook. The forest is full of dangers so please remain here." Savitri said, "I do not feel exhausted or weak after fasting and have made up my mind to come with you. Please, do not try to prevent me!"

"'The couple set out on their way and Savitri was delighted

by the natural beauty of the forest, which abounded in pea-cocks and other beautiful birds. Satyavan said to her, "Just look at the currents of these sacred rivers and the beauty of these fine trees decked with flowers". Savitri's mind, however, was preoccupied with Narada's words, knowing that the time was imminent.

"'Together they picked fruit and as Satyavan was cutting some branches, he began to perspire; his head started to ache and he became overcome with pain. He said, "Savitri, my head, limbs and heart are hurting, I feel as if my head has been pierced with hundreds of arrows. I need to go to sleep for I no longer have the energy to stand up." Savitri embraced her husband and sat on the ground, cradling his head gently on her lap. Once more Narada's words entered into her mind for she felt that the time she dreaded had come.

"'Suddenly she saw a large being cloaked in red approach-ing. His head was bedecked with silk cloth, signifying his royal status. He was as effulgent as the sun but with dark skin and terrifying red eyes; ominously, he carried a noose in his hand. He stood and stared at Satyavan but when Savit-ri became aware of his terrifying presence, she gently placed her husband's head on the ground and stood up to offer a respectful greeting. With a trembling voice she said, "It is quite obvious that you are no mere mortal so I assume that you are a deity. Please tell me who you are and what your intention is."

"'The mighty being then replied to her in the gravest tones, "Savitri, you are extremely devoted to your hus-band, and because your every deed is worthy of praise I am speaking with you. You should know that I am Yama, Lord of Death, and that Satyavan's days are over. I have come to bind him with this noose and take him away to the realm of the dead."

"'Savitri said, "It is said that you send your emissaries to take away the souls of mortals, so why have you come in person?" Yama replied, "This prince is adorned with numerous admirable qualities and was an ocean of virtue; he deserved to be treated with respect and for this reason I have come personally to take him." Then Yama exerted his power to draw Satyavan's soul from his body and bound him in the noose, bringing him under his complete control. When Satyavan's body was thus deprived of life, no longer breathing and completely still, Yama began to carry his departed soul away to the south. Overwhelmed by grief, Savitri began to follow him until Yama turned and said, "Stop following me, Savitri! Be on your way and perform the prescribed funeral duties. You no longer have any connection with this person and you have truly come as far as it is possible to travel in my company."

20. Savitri said, "'Wherever my husband is taken or wherever he chooses to go, I must go too. This is the eternal dharma (*sanatana-dharma*).

21. And because of the austerities I have performed, the respect I have shown for my teachers, the love I have for my husband and your grace upon me, my path should not be obstructed.

22. Those who are enlightened (*buddha*) and understand truth say that seven steps taken together makes two people friends. So now, on the basis of our friendship, I will say something to you. Please listen to what I say.

23. Persons who have achieved self-mastery make their

home in the forest, adhering to dharma and accepting the discomfort of this lifestyle. On the basis of their wisdom they teach the way of dharma. Therefore righteous people assert that dharma is supreme.

24. That one true expression of dharma is shown through the understanding of the righteous and everyone must adhere to this path. I have no desire for a second or a third way. Therefore righteous people assert that dharma is supreme."'

25. Yama said, "'Go back now. I am pleased by your words, with their pure enunciation of each letter, their allusions and their clear reasoning. So now choose any gift you may wish for, apart from the life of this man here. I will give you anything you ask for, O blameless one."'

26. Savitri said, "'My father-in-law has been deprived of his kingdom and now lives as a blind man in his ashram in the forest. Through your grace, may that king regain his sight and become powerful once more with splendour like that of fire or the sun."'

27. Yama said, "'I grant you this gift in full, O blameless one. Exactly what you have asked for will come to pass. You are fatigued by this journey so stop here and go back now; do not weary yourself further."'

28. Savitri said, "'How can there be any exhaustion when I am in the company of my husband? My path must surely take me wherever my husband goes, so I go wherever you take him. And now, O lord of the gods, listen again to what I have to say.

29. Even one encounter with righteous persons is the

most desirable thing and it is well known that friendship with such persons is even better. An encounter with a righteous person will never be fruitless and so one should live in a place where the righteous dwell.'"

30. Yama said, "'The words you have spoken are pleasing to the mind, they enlighten even the enlightened ones and they are highly beneficial. So now, my dear, you may ask from me a second gift, except for the life of this Satyavan.'"

31. Savitri said, "'My wise father-in-law was previously deprived of his kingdom. May that king now recover his domain and may that respected elder of mine never again have to give up the dharma he was born to follow. This is the second gift I ask of you.'"

32. Yama said, "'The king will very soon regain his kingdom and he will never again be deprived of his own dharma. Now that I will enact your desire, O princess, you should stop here and go back; do not weary yourself further.'"

33. Savitri said, "'It is in accordance with the rule of life that you subdue these living beings and it is because of this rule rather than your wish that you carry them away. It is for this reason, O lord, that you are known by the name of Yama ("'subduer'"). Now listen further to the words I have to say.

34. Showing no malice towards any living being through actions, thoughts or words; showing kindness to all and giving in charity—this is the eternal dharma, the *sanatana-dharma*, as defined by the righteous.

35. This is what the world is like: most men possess some strength in such matters but the righteous show compassion even towards their enemies."'

36. Yama said, "'The words you speak are as welcome as water to a person parched with thirst. So now, pure-hearted girl, you may ask from me any gift you desire, except for the life of this Satyavan.'"

37. Savitri said, "'That ruler of the earth who is my father has no sons. So let my father have a hundred sons as his own direct offspring so that his family line may be perpetuated. This is the third gift I ask of you.'"

38. Yama said, "'O pure-hearted girl, your father will have one hundred powerful sons who will perpetuate his line. Your wish is granted, princess, so now you should stop here; you have journeyed far along this path.'"

39. Savitri said, "'It does not seem far to me for I am in the company of my husband and my mind is hurrying even further on ahead. So as you continue on your way listen again to the words I will speak to you.

40. You are the mighty son of Vivasvan and it is for this reason that you are known as Vaivasvata by men of wisdom. It is through dharma and peacefulness that living beings invoke your favour and therefore, O lord, you are known in this world as the *dharmaraja*.

41. One does not place as much trust in oneself as one does in the righteous, so everyone especially wishes for friendship with such persons.

42. It is because of their attitude of goodwill that such

trust arises and hence any person will only place his trust in persons who are righteous.'"

43. Yama said, "'Never have I heard words such as those I have heard you speak here, O woman of beauty. I am pleased by this speech so now, except for the life of this person, choose a fourth blessing and then go on your way.'"

44. Savitri said, "'Then let there be a hundred sons born directly from myself and Satyavan to continue both our lines, and may they all be endowed with strength and heroism. This is the fourth boon I ask from you.'"

45. Yama said, "'You will indeed beget a hundred sons endowed with strength and heroism and they will bring you joy. Now weary yourself no more; stop here for you have come too far along this path.'"

46. Savitri said, "'The righteous are constant in their adherence to dharma; the righteous never become dejected, nor do they waver in their commitment; when the righteous meet with other righteous persons the meeting is never fruitless; the righteous have nothing to fear from other righteous persons.

47. Through their truthfulness the righteous cause the sun to move; through their austerity the righteous sustain the earth; the righteous dictate the course of the past and the future, O king; the righteous are never discouraged in the midst of righteous persons.

48. Knowing the eternal nature of this mode of conduct as it is followed by noble persons, the righteous take action on behalf of others without expecting anything in return.

49. Amongst righteous persons no act of mercy is ever futile; no profit or honour is ever lost in this way. And because this rule is always adhered to by the righteous, the righteous thus become the protectors of all.'"

50. Yama said, "'As you speak more and more on the subject of dharma, your sweet words delight the mind for they are full of great meaning and I become increasingly devoted to you. O you who adhere so closely to your vows, please now choose a gift that is beyond compare.'"

51. Savitri said, "'You cannot fulfil the gift already given without granting this next wish of mine. Therefore, O bestower of honour, the gift I ask for amongst all other gifts is that this Satyavan be restored to life for without my husband I am like one who is herself dead.

52. Without my husband I have no desire for happiness. Without my husband I have no desire for heaven. Without my husband I have no desire for wealth. Bereft of my husband I have no determination to live.

53. You have already granted me the gift of a hundred sons and yet you are depriving me of my husband. So now the gift I ask for is that this Satyavan may live so that your word may be true.

You granted me a hundred children yet you take my husband from me; so I ask for this one wish: restore Satyavan's life and bring truth to your words."

"'Then Yama, the dispenser of justice, untied the noose and with a cheerful heart said to Savitri, "You are the most blessed lady for I have set him free! He is now yours and free from illness. He will attain great success and will live for four hundred years. Celebrating rituals and rites he will become famous throughout the world and together you will have one hundred sons. These warriors, along with their children and grandchildren, will always be kings and always be famously connected with your name. Your father's children will resemble the celestial beings and will also become famous for their glory." Having granted these wishes to Savitri and finally appeasing her, Yama departed for his own abode. Savitri then returned to the spot where she had left her husband's ashen corpse. Upon seeing him lying on the ground she sat down and once more placed his head in her lap. Slowly Satyavan regained consciousness and opened his eyes, looking affectionately into the eyes of his beloved Savitri. Just like a person who has been travelling to strange places and returned home after a long time, he addressed her saying, "I have been asleep for a long time! Why did you not wake me? Where is that strange person who was dragging me away?" To this Savitri said, "You have indeed slept for a long time on my lap. The restrainer of living beings, Yama himself, has now gone away and you are renewed. Now, if you are able, stand up and take a look around and behold the dark night that has come upon us."

"'Having regained his consciousness, Satyavan stood up like somebody who had just enjoyed a very good sleep, and seeing himself in the woods he said, "O Savitri, I came with you to get fruit and while I was cutting wood I felt a pain in my head. So intense was this pain that I could not even stand up. I remember lying on your lap and you embracing me before I lost my senses. It was dark everywhere but then I saw a person with bright effulgence. Do you know anything about this? Was it a dream or was it reality?"' Savitri responded, "It is very late, I shall explain everything to you tomorrow."

In this way Savitri saved her beloved from the clutches of death through her wisdom and her deep understanding of the nature of dharma. Even Yama himself was amazed by the depths of her knowledge and became indebted to her because of the beauty of the words she spoke.'"

It is apparent from this wonderful narrative and the translated verses in particular that Savitri is a woman who possesses both wisdom and a keen intellect. One might even say that there is a bit of cunning about her although one cannot help but suspect that by the end Yama is willing to fall for the trap she sets him. But beyond that representation of an enlightened woman and a loving wife, we might pay particular attention to the way in which she defines the *sanatana* or "'eternal'" dharma. Verse 34 seems particularly significant in this regard for it is here that she gives a direct interpretation of what is meant by *sanatana-dharma*: to be entirely free of malice, to show kindness and compassion at all times and to give charity to those in need. We might note as well that in 31 she mentions her father's *sva-dharma* ("'own'" dharma) as something he has been deprived of. What she means is that people may have a dharma or duty that is specific to their own position in life, in this case the specific dharma of her father-in-law is to rule his kingdom in the proper way for the good of the citizens. But the *sanatana-dharma* goes beyond this *sva-dharma* as it is universal in the sense that it is for all people at all times, regardless of their background or social position.

She also speaks frequently about the "'righteous'" people and the manner in which they conduct themselves. The actual word used here in Sanskrit is *sat* and although "'righteous'" may not entirely capture the literal meaning it probably comes as close as any other English equivalent. What the word *sat* really refers to here is one who does things properly and is correct in his or her conduct. Savitri suggests that such persons are favourably inclined towards everyone they encounter, even those who may be inimical towards them. Hence they are persons one can trust and rely on and in whom one can place one's confidence. They do good towards others not out of any hope of reward, but simply because it is the right thing to do, and because of this mode of conduct they are referred to here as *rakshitris*, those who will give protection to others in times of need.

So as well as this being such a wonderful story, which has been retold countless times in books, comics, films, dance and drama, the words of Savitri give us a really important insight into what we are to understand by the concept of dharma and the dharmic way of living. It is as much an outlook on life as it is a code of conduct, but where that benign and kindly disposition is translated into direct action, then that action takes the form of deeds that give shelter and protection to any living being in need. The phrase *sanatana -dharma* is often used amongst Hindus today and it is frequently suggested as an alternative designation to "'Hinduism'", but here we see a clear statement as to what *sanatana -dharma* actually means. Although some religious people might share its values, it is not really any sort of religion at all but rather a disposition of absolute goodwill towards all other beings and the attempt to act for their benefit and well-being. And in this sense we can see that the concept of dharma expressed here by Savitri is really rather similar to the idea that Krishna gave us through his conversation with Arjuna when the latter was resolved on killing his own brother.

7

A Thousand Years of Fun

*Happiness is never found through selfish desires. In fact,
what I have found is that selfish cravings only increase our
desires, similar to how the sacrificial fire flames up when
butter is poured into it.*
King Yayati, Mahabharata

*Our economy is based on spending billions to persuade peo-
ple that happiness is buying things, and then insisting that
the only way to have a viable economy is to make things for
people to buy so they'll have jobs and get enough money to
buy things.*
Philip Elliot Slater

Another insightful narrative from the Adi-parvan of the
Mahabharata is that of King Yayati. His simple yet profound
message that no amount of wealth or material pleasure can
bring us contentment is one that we all understand but often
becomes lost in the midst of so many distractions.

The great King Yayati, the son of Nahusha, was once
cursed by his father-in-law, a powerful Brahmana priest
called Usanas, because he fell in love with his wife's best
friend. The terrible curse was such that within a short pe-
riod he would be overcome with decrepitude, weakness,
and old age. In a state of anxiety, Yayati cried out, "'But I am
not yet finished being a young man! There is still so much I
wish to enjoy, especially with my young and beautiful wife
Devayani. I beg you to take away this curse of decrepitude,
keeping old age a distant thought.'" Thinking of his daugh-

ter's position, the saint Usanas said to the king, "'I never tell a lie, O King, and it is clear you have already started to suffer from the effects of the curse; but if it is what you desire, I will allow you to transfer this curse to another person.'" Yayati replied, "'Thank you, I will do as you have advised and transfer this curse to whichever one of my loyal sons is prepared to give me the gift of his youth. In return I shall present him with the whole kingdom, and he will be famous across the world for his virtue and his devotion to his parents.'" Usanas said, "'Just think of me and you will be able to transfer the curse to whoever you wish. Certainly, whichever son takes on this affliction deserves to be on the throne. He will surely become famous everywhere for taking on such a curse.'"

Overcome with anguish and the burden of old age, the distressed king returned to his capital and summoned his eldest son, the accomplished Yadu, and said to him, "'Dear son, I have been cursed with old age by Devayani's father, Usanas. Just look how my skin has become wrinkled and my hair is completely white. This misfortune is overwhelming me for I still desire the enjoyment of youth. Would you, my dear son, take this decrepitude and weakness from me so that I would be able to enjoy your youth? I promise to return your youth back to you after a thousand years have passed.'"

Yadu replied, "'Old age is both inconvenient and undesirable, father, for even eating or drinking properly become difficult for the elderly. For this reason I cannot take on your decrepitude. Having white hair, being cheerless and dull, with wrinkles all over the body, along with deformities, weak limbs, inability to work, emaciation, and being easily defeated by all: these are the consequences I would have to endure and therefore I do not accept. O King, you have other sons who have always been dearer to you than me so ask one of them to take on your curse."' Yayati angrily replied, "'You originated from my heart but will not even fulfil my appeal. Because you disobey me, your children shall never be Kings."'

Then he summoned another of his sons and said to him, "'O Turvasu, would you take my old age and weakness from me? With your youth I wish to enjoy the pleasures of life. After a thousand years I will return to take back my decrepitude from you."' Turvasu replied, "'I cannot stand weakness, Father, for it takes away every type of enjoyment. I would no longer have an appetite for pleasures, and would be bereft of strength, beauty and intellect. In effect, my life would be gone."' Yayati hastily retorted, "'Now I see that this child born from my heart will not accept what I ask of him. Turvasu, your race shall never last. You foolish boy, you shall be the king of those who are impure, living with people who survive by eating rotten food, who are inherently mean-spirited and who are sinful and completely ignoble."'

Having cursed his son for not accepting his request, King Yayati then summoned another son, saying, "'O Drahyu, will you take a thousand years of old age from your dear father by gifting me your youth?"' Drahyu said, "'Father, one who is old and weak cannot ride elephants, horses and chariots. I would not be able to enjoy the company of women, either. I am sorry but I also do not wish to take up your request."' Yayati was so frustrated by his son's refusal that he cried, "'You are royalty only in name! Now call Anu, my beloved son."' When Anu, his fourth son, came before him, Yayati made the same request, "'Please take on my decrepitude."' Just like his brothers, however, Anu could not bear the thought of giving up his youth, "'I cannot imagine eating like a child,"' he said, "'and no longer being able to worship the sacrificial fire, and being beset by so many other problems. I cannot see how anyone would ever agree to such a difficult request.'"

Yayati's last hope was his youngest child, Puru, to whom he said, "'Puru, although you are the youngest, you are dearest to me. White hair, wrinkled skin and old age have got the better of me and this has all happened due to a curse by Usanas. Puru, I have not yet fulfilled my desires in life and now you alone can provide the solution to my plight. Please take the burden of this curse and I promise to return your youth after a thousand years have passed.'" Puru said, "'You are my father, I would do anything for you, so of course you can have my youth.'" To this Yayati replied, "'You have great humility and have pleased me so much. I know that the people in your kingdom will be blessed with everything they desire.'"

Relieved, Yayati quickly brought his father-in-law to mind, and miraculously his old age was transferred to his noble-minded son, Puru, the youngest of the five brothers. With his rejuvenated youth, Yayati began to indulge in the best of life's pleasures, his heart filled with delight. He lived life to the full but still conducted himself virtuously, performing religious rites and being kind and hospitable to all. He achieved every object of his desire and travelled to exotic locations with beautiful women, enjoying everything a man could wish for. Then, after a thousand years of lustful indulgence had passed, Yayati slowly returned to Puru's kingdom and addressed the son who had freed him from decrepitude and old age, 'My son,' he said, 'you have given me the gift of your youth and I have relished all the pleasures life has to offer. Every possible desire a man could have was hunted down and enjoyed by me.'

'But what I have understood after these thousand years have elapsed is that our happiness is never truly fulfilled by such selfish indulgence. In fact, it is just the opposite. Enjoying pleasures of this type serves only to increase our desires, just as the sacrificial fire blazes higher when butter is poured into it. I have realised that even if someone came to possess the whole earth with all her beautiful fields of rice and barley, all her silver and gold, all her precious gems and animals, still he would not find satisfaction. This craving for sensual pleasure should therefore be controlled. True happiness belongs only to one who remains free of such selfish longings but this is so difficult for the wicked and unethical to achieve. This state of discontented longing continues through one life after another and is the real difficulty humanity faces. For a thousand years my heart has pursued everything I sought after and I have enjoyed unlimited pleasures, but this thirst for more has simply increased day by day with no sign of its ever being quenched.

'Therefore I have decided to take a different path; I shall fix my mind on *Brahman* and peacefully pass the rest of my days in company with the innocent deer in the forest. Puru, I cannot express how pleased I am by your actions. Take back your youth now and may you always prosper. The kingdom is yours to rule; all the land between the two rivers Ganga and Yamuna is yours. This indeed is the central region of the Earth and only the outlying regions will be ruled by your brothers. Those without anger are superior to those caught under its sway; those with a forgiving disposition are always superior to the unforgiving. Humans have a greater responsibility than animals, and amongst humans those educated have a still greater responsibility. If somebody acts wickedly towards you, my child, you should forbear and merely return the wrong to them. If you allow anger to flourish, it will burn your very self; it is anger that takes away a person's good qualities. You should never cause pain to others by speaking vicious and cruel words. Never seek to control your enemies by despicable methods. Never utter the kind of malicious and scorching words that can torture others, for he who pricks others with the sharp thorn of his cruel words lives as if he has demons in his mouth. True prosperity flies away from the very sight of such a person.

'You should always keep virtuous people as your role models; you should always compare your actions to the acts of those virtuous people and forever disregard the actions and words of the wicked. You should always make the conduct of the wise the model to live your own life by. When a person is hurt by the vicious arrows of horrible words, even though they may be hurled unintentionally, they can cause people to suffer day and night. Indeed, these words strike a place much deeper than the body. Therefore, my son, the wise ones never hurl this type of arrow. There is no means by which the people of the world can worship the gods that is superior to kindness, friendship, charity, and sweet words to every living being. So my dear child, you should always utter words that soothe rather than scorch, and you should always give praise to the praiseworthy. Always be quick to give but reluctant to take away. What you have suffered on my behalf, Puru, can never be repaid.' Then, after bestowing the kingdom on his youngest son, the wise King Yayati retired happily to the forest.

By the simple yet powerful account of the life of King Yayati we can remind ourselves of how often we selfishly pursue the objects of our desires, even when we know they will not truly make us happy. As Yayati asserts so eloquently,

'They are just like pouring butter into a fire.' The thousand years of chasing his desires did not satisfy Yayati, and it is equally the case that whatever wealth we may acquire in life, it will never seem to be enough.

Yayati's words on non-violence express a similar view to that of Gandhi who famously pointed out that the rule of 'an eye for an eye' makes the whole world blind; and in the end the king finds contentment only in human virtue. In another wonderful speech later on in the same chapter he says, 'The way to success and happiness is through having control over desires, a tranquil mind, self-command, modesty, simplicity, and by showing kindness to all living beings. These can all be lost by vanity. The man who after acquiring knowledge comes to regard himself as clever and learned does not achieve the true goals of life, for this type of knowledge is not enough to become one with *Brahman*. Of course studying, worship, and other practises are important but if they are mixed with vanity they only cause further problems. The good alone will take care of goodness; the wicked will never be concerned. I have done this; they think ""I have studied so much, given so much to charity and achieved so much"", but this is exactly the type of vanity that should never be entertained.' King Yayati's message has been carried down the ages and it is just as relevant today as it was thousands of years ago.

8

Ashoka, from Great to Good

*Now it is conquest by Dhamma that the Beloved-of-the-Gods
considers to be the best conquest.*
Ashoka's Rock Edict No.13 (S. Dhammika)

*Darkness cannot drive out darkness; only light can do that.
Hate cannot drive out hate; only love can do that.*
Martin Luther King, Jr.

Ashoka was a mighty emperor of the Mauryan dynasty in India. Scholars of Indian history suggest that he lived from 304 to 232 BC. His conquests lead him rule much of India: his vast kingdom stretched from the Hindu Kush Mountains of Afghanistan to modern day Bangladesh. Legend has it that Ashoka was so evil that he slaughtered his own brothers to take the throne and in this same vicious spirit subjugated and dominated many new provinces for the empire he inherited from his father. One may feel that history is littered with wicked monarchs who massacre innocent people and conquer lands, but with Ashoka it was different. His life took an unusual turn that is very relevant to our dialogue on dharma. Below is a translation from one of the many edicts he had set in stone throughout his kingdom, some of which can still be seen to this day.

After eight years on the throne, the Beloved of the Gods, the King Piyadasi, conquered the region of Kalinga. A hundred and fifty thousand people were exiled, a hundred thousand were killed, and many times that number deceased. After all of this, now that Kalinga was conquered, the Beloved of the

Gods very earnestly practised dharma, desired dharma and taught dharma. On annexing Kalinga, the Beloved of the Gods felt remorse for the suffering caused, for when an independent country is conquered, the slaughter, death, and exile of people were extremely painful to the Beloved of the Gods and it weighed heavily on his mind. What is even more deplorable to the Beloved of the Gods is that the citizens who lived in that country, whatever class or sect they belonged to, who were obedient to their superiors, obedient to their parents, obedient to their teachers, and kind and devoted to their friends, acquaintances, colleagues, family and servants, all suffer from the violence, killing and being separated from the ones they love. Participating in this suffering weighs heavily on the mind of the Beloved of the Gods. (Ashokas 13th Major Rock Edict, adapted from the translation of Romila Thapar in *Asoka and the Decline of the Mauryas*, OUP, 1997.))

After a major military conquest that engulfed a significant part of India through unimaginable violence, the emperor Ashoka was overcome with remorse and compassion and was revolted by his own actions. He issued such edicts throughout the country, communicating his new vision of love, tolerance and compassion. All over India his messages can be found providing us with a unique insight into this ancient king's radical change of heart.

His new duty in life was to do his upmost to serve his people in every way he could. The philosophy put forth is not dogmatic but promotes meta-ethical precepts such as humility, honesty, kindness, truthfulness, and compassion for all living beings. The philanthropic ruler went on to build hospitals, promote vegetarianism, plant countless trees, wells and shelters, and provided food and water for the underprivileged.

Ashoka's reign focused on ahimsa (non-violence) and included provision for animals as well as humans. He urged every one of his citizens to abstain from butchery and to practise non-violence as much as possible, and even went to the extent of making watering fountains specifically for animals. Although Ashoka's is definitely an extreme example, for not many are likely to rule large sections of the earth as he did, his discontent after pursuing his own self-interest at the expense of others is something most will be able to appreciate. His shift in consciousness may have provided the impetus for the rise of Buddhist thought but his focus on ahimsa and compassion have left a legacy throughout India, which in the modern era provided inspiration for the likes of Vivekananda, Gandhi and other reforming leaders.

We can all start to realise the impact dharma can have in our lives, in the modern day as well, not just in the lives of ancient Indians. Philanthropic and charitable organisations like that founded by Bill and Melinda Gates have worked tirelessly and with great success to help eradicate disease and poverty in India. The Akshayapatra foundation has now provided over a billion meals to help keep disadvantaged children in school, whilst Nelson Mandela through his Truth and Reconciliation Committee forgave countless people for the tyranny of apartheid. We may not have the ability to bring about such radical changes but even the humblest act of kindness can become a profound catalyst for a butterfly effect of dharma. Although it will always be difficult to codify dharma, we can certainly establish the ideals of positive meta-ethics. At the beginning of Chapter Sixteen of the Bhagavad-gita, Krishna presents Arjuna with a list of divine qualities and characteristics that virtuous people display.

1. Fearlessness, purification of one's nature, remaining resolute in the pursuit of knowledge through yoga practice; charity, self-control, performing duties, recitation of the Vedas, austerity, honesty;
2. Not harming, truthfulness, avoiding anger, renunciation, tranquillity, never maligning others, compassion for other beings, being free of greed, kindness, modesty, never wavering;
3. Energy, patience, resolve, purity, the absence of malice and of arrogance; these constitute the godly disposition, O Bharata.

It becomes apparent from Krishna's list that the majority of these attributes are of the type that can provide the foundation that will allow us to make our own decisions on how to act properly. Interestingly, Krishna then goes on to outline the attributes of those who deviate from virtue, and speaks of the cruel deeds they perform, which lead to the 'destruction of the earth' (16.8). 'Bound by the ropes of their aspirations, dominated by desire and anger, they accumulate wealth by immoral means in order to fulfil their desires'(16.12). Krishna goes on to include self-importance, stubbornness, being dominated by wealth, pride and passion, egotism, arrogance, desire and hatred as the *asuric* ('demonic') qualities displayed by those who deviate from virtue.

There are numerous similar lists of positive and negative traits throughout Indian literature, in the Upanishads, Mahabharata and Puranas, describing how Hindus have defined virtue over thousands of years. The Chandogya Upanishad, for example, tells us about King Janasruti who was famous throughout the land for building feeding halls for the hungry and poor, giving generously to all. In reality we might see both good and bad forces within ourselves, pulling our actions back and forth, but we all have the capability of working towards a disposition of righteousness as described by Krishna and by the Ashokan Edicts. Ashoka was a prime example of an individual who transformed his disposition from *asuric* to *sattvic*, or good, and it is this shift of focus from self-interest to the duty of morality that characterises a dharmic person.

9

The Other Side of the Coin

Like a charioteer using the whip, he should seek to bring all regions under his control, seeking to take hold of the effulgent prosperity of his enemy.
Duryodhona, Mahabharata

Greed, for lack of a better word, is good. Greed is right. Greed works. Greed clarifies and cuts through to the essence of the evolutionary spirit.
Gordon Gekko, Wall Street

The Mahabharata is a great work in many ways but in particular for the manner in which it reveals its most profound lessons through narrative and characterisation. At the heart of the narrative are two major characters, Yudhishthira and Duryodhana, the former epitomising dharma and the problems of its implementation, whilst Duryodhana offers a dark antithesis to Yudhishthira, not in any monstrous fashion but in a manner that is all too familiar from the real world we live in. So let us now continue our exploration of dharma by looking at the lives, characters and beliefs of these two principal personalities. Let us start first with Duryodhana so that we can understand the view of life that stands in constant opposition to the ideal of dharma espoused by Yudhishthira and made evident throughout his life.

This passage comes from the Mahabharata's second book, the Sabha-parvan, literally 'the section describing what happened in the assembly halls'. At this point Duryodhana is depressed to see the prosperity of Yudhishthira and his other cousins and is constantly unhappy about the situation he finds himself in. His father, Dhritarashtra, attempts to console him by pointing out that he has just as much power as Yudhishthira and can match whatever wealth his cousin is seen to possess, hence there is no need for anguish or envy. He further explains that greatness is shown when one never covets the wealth or possessions of others and is content with one's own prosperity— Duryodhana should regard Yudhishthira as a friend and ally so that they can present a powerful united front against all hostile outsiders. In response to this sagacious advice from his father, Duryodhana makes the following reply:

'Although you know many things, still you confound me as we are linked together like one boat tied to others. Why is it that you do not seek our own interests? Or is it simply that you hate me, father? I am not the leader of your party for it is you who are their instructor, but you always speak about a goal that may be realised sometime in the future. If a person is led astray by the other faction then his confusion will take him away from the right course of action. How then can his associates follow him down that path? You, O King, are full of wisdom, you show due respect to the words of the ancients and your senses are under control, but you are causing us confusion when we are already set on the goals we aim to achieve. Brihaspati has taught that the ways of kings are different from the type of conduct suitable for other persons, for a ruler must always think of his own interest and make endeavours accordingly.

'The way of the ruling class, Great King, is to be intent on victory. Whether it be dharma or adharma, this is the proper way for a ruler to proceed, O Best of the Bharatas. Like a charioteer using the whip he should seek to bring all regions under his control, seeking to take hold of the effulgent prosperity of his enemy. Those who properly understand the art of weapons assert that a weapon is a course of action, concealed or displayed, which damages one's enemy. It is not simply an instrument that cuts another person.

'Being discontented is the very root of prosperity and therefore I do not wish to be content with what I have. He who constantly endeavours for the highest position is certainly the best of leaders, O King. Others will surely seize what one has previously acquired, for this type of aggressive action is what is known as the *raja-dharma*, the dharma of kings. Sakra cut off Namuchi's head after making an agreement not to attack him, for he understood that this is the ancient mode of conduct in relation to an enemy. Like a snake eating an animal that lives in a hole, the earth will swallow these two: a king who does not take hostile action and a Brahmana who never leaves his home.

'No one is a person's enemy by birth, O Lord of the People. It is one whose conduct in life is the same as one's own who is one's enemy and no one else. Anyone who foolishly disregards the growing power of a rival faction will be cut down at the root just like a person afflicted by the spread of a disease. However insignificant an enemy might appear to be, if he is allowed to continually expand his power he will swallow you up, just as an anthill can destroy a whole tree at its root.

'So never be content to observe the prosperity of a rival. For the wise this type of policy is a burden that has to be borne on the head. Just as the body naturally grows stronger from the moment of birth, so a person who seeks to expand his own prosperity must thrive in the midst of his family members, for it is power that ensures such expansion. I have not yet been able to seize the opulence of the Pandavas and hence I am beset by misgivings. Either I will take possession of their wealth or I will fall down and die on the battlefield. If I cannot become their equal then I have no desire to live, O Lord of the People. The Pandavas are constantly expanding whilst we remain as we are.'

Now, by way of contrast, let us consider the way that Yudhishthira conducts himself in relation to those who have wronged him. In Book 3 of the Mahabharata, we find Yudhishthira and his brothers stripped of sovereignty and forced to live as exiles in the forest. During this time their wife Draupadi is seized and carried away by another king named Jayadratha who is full of desire to enjoy her beauty. After the kidnapping, Yudhishthira's two younger brothers, Bhima and Arjuna, pursue and capture Jayadratha and release Draupadi from his grasp. The enraged Bhima wishes to strike down the abductor for his mistreatment of a woman who spurned his advances, but Yudhishthira is rather more conciliatory. Here is the account of the capture and release of Jayadratha as narrated in Chapter 256 of Book 3 of the Mahabharata:

On seeing Bhima and Arjuna approaching him, weapons in hand, Jayadratha fled into the forest in order to save his life. Bhima, however, pursued his adversary, caught him by the hair and threw him to the ground before beating and kicking him. When Jayadratha lost consciousness as a result of this assault, Arjuna intervened and said to his elder brother, 'Stop now and act as Yudhishthira directed. Do not make our cousin Duhsala a widow.'

Bhima replied, 'This lowest of men who has dared to threaten Draupadi in this way does not deserve to live. Why should I always have to follow the instruction of our overly merciful brother? You also are always holding me back with your childish ideas.' He then took a razor-sharp arrow and shaved Jayadratha's head leaving only five tufts. 'If you wish to save your life,' he said to him, 'then you must go to the court of every king in the land and announce that you are the slave of the Pandava brothers.'

Desiring to save his own life, Jayadratha replied, 'I will do so,' and fell silent. Bhima then bound him tightly, placed him on his chariot and took him to Yudhishthira who was waiting with Draupadi and the sages who accompanied him. When Yudhishthira saw Jayadratha bound and blood-ied, he could not help but laugh at him, but then said, 'Now release this man.' To this Bhima replied, 'Very well, but you should tell Draupadi that this worthless fool is now the slave of the Pandavas.'

Speaking mildly out of consideration for his enraged brother, Yudhishthira then said, 'Please accept my instruc-tion and let him go free.' Understanding Yudhishthira's disposition and glancing in his direction, Draupadi agreed with this decision, saying, 'Set this slave free, for you have already shaved his head leaving only five tufts.'

When Jayadratha was released he offered his respects to Yudhishthira and the sages who surrounded him. Then the compassionate Yudhishthira, the son of Dharma, addressed these words to Jayadratha, 'Depart now as a free man but never act in such a way again. I condemn you for your lust for women; you are low-minded and are surrounded by oth-er vile companions. Who other than yourself, the lowest of men, could act in such a way?'

Seeing that perpetrator of wicked deeds in an almost life-less state, the Lord of the Bharatas then expressed his com-passion towards him. 'May your understanding of dharma now grow stronger' he said, 'and your inclination towards adharma cease. Depart now, Jayadratha, with your horses, chariots and soldiers. I wish you good fortune.' Addressed in this way and with his face turned downwards in shame, Jayadratha departed in silence and journeyed to Gangadvara, the mouth of the Ganga, with sorrow in his heart.

Now let us consider one more incident that reveals Yudhishthira's disposition and his understanding of dharma. After the final battle is over and the Pandavas have emerged triumphant over Duryodhana and his allies, there is another difference of opinion between Yudhishthira and Bhima, this time over the attitude they should adopt towards Dhritarashtra, the blind father of Duryodhana who had repeatedly taken his son's side in his persecution of the Pandavas. Bhima despised his aged uncle and wanted him to pay for his wrongdoing but again Yudhishthira's attitude was very different. The following passage is a summation of the content of the first ten chapters of Book 15 of the Mahabharata.

After their victory in the Kurukshetra war the Pandavas began to reign over the kingdom with Yudhishthira as the undisputed monarch of the realm. Without any sense of malice or desire for revenge, Yudhishthira always showed the greatest respect towards Dhritarashtra, the father of Duryodhana, and supplied him with all the luxuries he was accustomed to enjoy. Sometimes Dhritarashtra acted as if he were himself the king, setting free prisoners and pardoning those convicted of crime, but never once did Yudhishthira say any word to object to this behaviour. Rather he insisted to his brothers that they must try to assuage the grief Dhritarashtra felt over the loss of his sons by acting towards him as if he were their own father.

Although Yudhishthira was entirely free of malice, the

same could not be said of his younger brother Bhima. This mighty warrior could neither forget nor forgive the injustices that had been inflicted upon them by Dhritarashtra and his sons, and recollection of the insults to Draupadi still provoked rage in his heart. Hence when Yudhishthira instructed his brothers to show only kindness and respect towards their blind uncle, Bhima accepted the order but not the mood of forgiveness on which it was based.

He then began to perform actions that were disturbing to Dhritarashtra. He used his own servants to secretly ensure that his uncle's instructions were not followed. Once whilst recalling the wickedness of Duryodhana he stated aloud in Dhritarashtra's hearing, 'All the sons of that blind king were killed by me with these two arms of mine. They had so many weapons and such vast armies but when they came within the grip of these mace-like arms of mine all of them were done to death.'

Being repeatedly afflicted by these and similar words of Bhima, Dhritarashtra and his wife Gandhari decided they would retire to the forest to live a life of religious austerity. Coming before Yudhishthira, the old king confessed that all the suffering, conflict and tragedy was his fault alone because of the foolish way in which he had given support to his worthless son Duryodhana. 'I now wish to atone for these sins,' he said, 'by living a life of penance and religious observance.'

Yudhishthira was distressed to hear his uncle speak in this way and begged him to stay a little while longer so that he might teach him about morality and how a king should rule his domain. Dhritarashtra agreed to do so and taught Yudhishthira at length about the science of kingship, but then again he stated his desire to depart for the forest. First, however, he wished to make offerings on behalf of his sons and the other family members who had fallen in battle so that they might find happiness in the afterlife.

Yudhishthira was happy to provide Dhritarashtra with all the wealth required for elaborate offerings to be made on behalf of his sons, but Bhima had a different opinion on the subject. Again it fell to Arjuna to try to conciliate between his two elder brothers urging Bhima to accept Yudhishthira's views on the basis of forgiveness and compassion. Bhima, however, would not be won over. 'It is we who should make offerings on behalf of the worthy elders of our family who fell in battle, not this Dhritarashtra. As for his sons, let them rot! Let them sink down to some degraded form of existence deprived of the offerings made on their behalf. This is all they deserve. How can you so easily forget the sufferings we were forced to endure and the wrongs that were done to us? Where were these elders and family members then?' On hearing this harsh speech, Yudhishthira rebuked his brother and asked him to be silent.

Yudhishthira then made arrangements for the offerings to be made by Dhritarashtra and asked him to forgive Bhima for the words he had spoken. Dhritarashtra then began to give gifts in charity on behalf of each of his sons and dead relatives, naming each in turn as the recipient of the reward to be won for an act of piety. And as his aged uncle gave away each gift or sum of money, Yudhishthira came forward and gave twice as much so that the acts of charity should be of unrivalled generosity.

Finally, here is a short passage that gives some insight into the way in which Yudhishthira ruled his kingdom and his attitude towards citizens in need. Again it is indicative of the way in which he is to be regarded as the very embodiment of dharma. This passage is taken from Book 12 (Chapter 42) of the Mahabharata, the Santi-parvan or book of peace, and describes how Yudhishthira began his reign after his triumph in battle.

9. Just as he had done previously, Yudhishthira paid his respects to Dhritarashtra, Gandhari, Vidura and all the other leading Kauravas along with their servants.

10. The kind-hearted King of the Kurus also paid his respects to those women who lost husbands or sons in the battle and offered them shelter.

11. Dedicating himself to the principle of not harming anyone, the mighty king displayed his kindness by providing the poor, the blind and the destitute with homes, clothing and food.

12. Having conquered the whole world and being free of enemies, King Yudhishthira at last found pleasure.

These passages give us further insights into the nature of dharma but at the same time they raise some rather uncomfortable questions. Although few would accept the full implications of Duryodhana's message, there is a genuine argument to suggest that the desire to achieve great things is not an unworthy aspiration and the display of ambition he refers to can provide an effective counter to inertia or complacency. The real problem arises when such sentiments become overwhelming or even obsessive to the point where any sense of virtue is seen as weakness and a barrier to success. In Duryodhana's case, he regards the competitive spirit as providing an impetus for success and will not allow any other principle to take precedence over his ambition. He also argues that the rules of morality for kings (or in our day political leaders) cannot be the same as those applied to other classes of people, which is another point we might not be able to dismiss entirely.

Where we turn to Yudhishthira, we can all admire his compassion, forgiveness and generosity of spirit but at the same time we may have misgivings about his willingness to excuse what is in Jayadratha's case a misdemeanour of the worst kind. Should criminals of this type who use their physical strength to oppress and brutalise women and children simply be let off with some minor words of admonition? Certainly Bhima does not think so and he is constantly frustrated by his elder brother's mild disposition, which he regards as inappropriate for a ruler whose responsibility is to administer justice. So on the one hand one might find the willingness to forgive an elderly relative worthy of emulation but at the same time we may have doubts about whether Yudhishthira's application of the principles of absolute virtue to government action is entirely appropriate or indeed practical. If your house is being broken into by a gang of violent criminals and you call for help, who would you rather have respond to your call, the energetic and aggressive Bhima or the mild and tolerant Yudhishthira?

The final point to note here is in relation to Yudhishthira's government and the concern he shows for those who are destitute and in need of help. There are numerous debates taking place at present over the responsibility of the state to provide for the needs of those unable to care fully for themselves. It is a difficult issue to resolve definitively but the point made here is very clear, namely that one's commitment to dharma, virtue and not harming is never merely passive or just some intellectual construct. It must have a practical application in terms of a commitment to act on behalf of those in need. As we can see from these brief extracts, the Mahabharata never offers its readers unrealistic answers to complex questions. The issue of the necessary use of vigorous action and even violent means is explored through the characters of Yudhishthira and his brother Bhima, but who is right? Yudhishthira is repeatedly referred to as *dharma-putra*, the son of Dharma, but at the same time we are forced to consider whether his unwavering addiction to pure virtue is practical for the world we live in. The Mahabharata rightly refrains from offering an overly simplistic response but rather it highlights the tension and the dilemma, and then asks us to use our honesty, integrity and intelligence to try to reach the right decision in any given situation.

10

The Golden Mongoose

*As long as one retains one's dedication to giving in charity,
one's dharma will never fade away. Through your virtue and
your adherence to the principles of dharma you have conquered the world and your fame will last forever.*
The Golden Mongoose, Mahabharata.

*It's an amazing thing to think that ours is the first generation
in history that really can end extreme poverty, the kind that
means a child dies for lack of food in its belly.*
Bono

We have chosen to include this passage because of its relevance to the question of religious and secular ethics. At
times religion insists on the primacy of the other world
over concern for people's welfare in the here and now. This
has been the case in India where the priestly class has often
appeared to be committed only to ritual actions and to be
uninterested in the welfare of the poor and oppressed. This
story from the Mahabharata reflects on this precise issue
and emerges with an (almost) unequivocal response. Here
the setting is again the aftermath of the great battle and we
find Yudhishthira filled with regret over the tragic loss of
life seeing himself as a sinful person because of the acts of
violence he has taken part in. The wise Vyasa comforts him
by insisting that everything that occurred was due to destiny alone and that he should perform an elaborate Vedic
ritual, which will serve as atonement for any sinful act he
may have performed.

Yudhishthira accepts this advice and arranges for the performance of an *asvamedha-yajna*, one of the most complex of the ritual ceremonies revealed in the Vedic scriptures. This ritual requires the participation of innumerable priests and is very costly to perform because of the golden implements used by the priests to make their offerings. Nonetheless, the necessary funding is obtained without recourse to additional taxation, and the rituals of atonement are all perfectly enacted. We join the story at the conclusion of the ceremony when Yudhishthira has just received the great blessing he has been seeking to eradicate any trace of sin. The passage here is a summation of the content of Chapter 92 of Book 14 of the Mahabharata.

Now hear about a most wonderful incident that occurred when the ritual was complete. After the priests had been rewarded and the poor and destitute all fed, a blue-eyed mongoose with a golden side suddenly appeared there and began to speak to Yudhishthira and his brothers. 'O you kings,' the mongoose said, 'this great ritual does not equal a small quantity of flour given away by a man who was about to break his fast.'

When they heard these words the priests came forward and began to question the extraordinary creature, 'Who are you? Where have you come from? How can you criticise the wonderful ceremony we have just completed? Every aspect of this ritual performance was perfectly enacted exactly as directed by the Vedas; the priests have been fully rewarded and generous gifts of charity have been given away. You appear very wise and you have a form like one of the gods, so please explain these words you have spoken.'

When he was questioned in this way, the mongoose replied as follows, 'In the sacred land of Kurukshetra there lived a pious Brahmana who fasted every day until the evening when he would take just a small quantity of simple food. There was then a famine in the land and the Brahmana and his family could never get enough to feed themselves. On some days they had nothing at all to eat. One day during this time of hardship, the Brahmana managed to obtain a quantity of flour barely sufficient to provide a meal for himself and his family.

The meal was prepared but just as the family were about to eat, a hungry guest arrived at their home begging for a morsel of food. All the family stood to welcome this stranger and respectfully requested him to come in and sit down. As the man was starving and on the verge of death each of them, beginning with the father, gave up his or her portion of the food and gave it to this man in order to ease his suffering. When the guest had eaten all the food available and the family was left with nothing, a light appeared in the sky, flowers rained down and Dharma, the god of virtue, descended to earth to bestow his blessings upon them.

Dharma spoke the following words, 'My blessings upon you, for your acts of kindness have made you glorious in this world and amongst the gods as well. As long as one retains one's dedication to giving in charity, one's dharma will never fade. Through your virtue and your adherence to the principles of dharma you have conquered the world and your fame will last forever.'

The Brahmana and his family then entered a celestial chariot and ascended to the realm of the gods. At that time I emerged from the hole where I lived and ran across the ground outside the Brahmana's house so that a few particles of the flour given in charity touched one side of my body. It is as a result of my contact with the food given in charity to a needy person that you see me now possessing this form with one side that is golden.

Now whenever I hear that religious acts are being undertaken I go to that place immediately in the hope that the whole of my body may become golden and it is for this reason that I have come here today. I remain, however, unchanged and it was for this reason that I stated earlier that the ceremony you have enacted here could not equal the simple act of charity performed by a man of kindness. It was due to the grains of flour that I became golden and clearly this great ritual, wonderful as it was, could not match the piety of those grains.' Having spoken these words, the mongoose became silent and disappeared from that place.

In the religions of the world this tension between ritual and pure virtue is often encountered and it becomes particularly acute when we find a person who has no interest in formal religion and yet is consistently charitable and benevolent towards others. In terms of the definition of dharma we are given here, such a person meets the criteria more fully than another who speaks constantly of religion but whose compassion towards others is less evident. The account of the golden mongoose presented above is clearly mythical and yet the point it makes is a significant one, which places virtue and compassion above even the most elaborate of ritual acts. This is what dharma really means, although it is interesting to note that at some later date an interpolation was added to the text of the Mahabharata, attempting to show that the mongoose was in fact an evil being who entered the sacrificial arena to spread doubt and confusion and thereby discredit the pristine Vedic religion. There can be little doubt that this addition to the text was made by some member of the priestly order unable to accept the precedence given to virtue over ritual, which the original text so clearly espouses. Overall we can see that the passage as it stands does not entirely dismiss the value of ritual acts but it is unequivocal in its assertion that compassion is the true heart of dharma.

11

Talking about Food

A wise man should therefore pursue the subtle science of dharma by performing his duty on the basis of authority. Not harming other beings is certainly recognised as superior to all other forms of dharma.
Bhisma, Mahabharata

All the arguments to prove man's superiority cannot shatter this hard fact: in suffering the animals are our equals.
Peter Singer

In the account of the speech of the golden mongoose we found that Yudhishthira was performing an elaborate Vedic fire ritual. Many will be aware that this type of ritual sometimes involved the slaughter of animals so that meat offerings could be made into the fire and this practice is referred to in relation to the ritual at which the mongoose appeared. We have already seen how ahimsa, or not harming, was repeatedly advocated as the very essence or defining characteristic of dharma and hence a further tension arises over ritual slaughter and indeed whether a person should eat meat as a part of his or her diet. We will consider the question of diet more fully in a later section but at this stage we might look again at the Mahabharata to see how the principle of not harming is applied to ritual slaughter and how non-violence is linked to the food we eat.

At the conclusion of the battle, in Book 12, The Book of Peace, Yudhishthira seeks guidance from Bhishma, his grandfather, on a whole range of subjects. At this time Bhishma is lying on the battlefield mortally wounded but still he is able to muster the strength to instruct Yudhishthira about kingship, morality and about the quest for liberation from rebirth. On various occasions Bhishma emphasises the respect that is due to the Brahmanas and the importance of ritual acts, but then Yudhishthira raises the specific question of whether or not a form of ritual that includes violence towards animals is acceptable. This discussion begins from Chapter 252 of Book 12 and again Yudhishthira's words are of interest for our consideration of dharma:

1. Yudhishthira said, 'You have explained that the marks of virtue indicative of dharma are subtle. But I have a specific instinct for such matters and can pronounce judgement based on inference.

2. You have already responded to many of the questions I had in mind. I will now say something more, O King, though not out of any desire to dispute your words.

3. The living beings of this world all give help to others in reaching their goal; they give them gifts and they go to their aid. It is not possible, Bharata, to understand dharma through a mere code of rules and regulations.

4. Dharma is one thing for one person whose affairs are flourishing and something else for a person facing difficulties. How is it possible to reach any conclusion about one's dharma in times of adversity by referring to a list of rules and regulations?

5. You also said that dharma is represented by the conduct of the righteous, but righteous persons are identified on the basis of their conduct. So how can anything be proved or disproved in this way, if there is no clear mark as to the conduct of the righteous?'

Here Yudhishthira is challenging the support Bhishma has shown for ritual and the priests who perform it but it is interesting to note again how the idea of tightly structured moral codes is challenged. Firstly, Yudhishthira states that he has an instinct for determining what is right or wrong and hence does not require a list of rules and prohibitions to guide his conduct, but then he points out that what is right and what is wrong will vary according to circumstances. This of course is the same point that Krishna made in one of our earlier passages but it is worth reflecting on again in light of what Yudhishthira is saying here. We should all know, for example, that theft or fraud are immoral acts because they bring suffering to the victim and are motivated by greed or selfish desire. This is certainly the case when we hear of shoplifting or salesmen defrauding people through misrepresentation of goods and services. But what about in the case of a poor man whose family is starving? If he steals a loaf of bread in order to feed his children are we certain that this is an immoral action? As Yudhishthira says here, the marks of dharma are rather subtle, and rigid codes of conduct can be a hindrance rather than a help.

Responding to Yudhishthira's objections, Bhishma appears to accept his point as he then proceeds to present a series of conversations between representatives of the priesthood and critics who condemn the violence of the rituals they perform. Here is a short example of the type of material we are talking about, which rejects the moral standing of any Vedic ritual that involves violence towards living beings. This is the *Vicakhnu-gita*, literally 'the proclamation of Vichakhnu', which appears as Chapter 257 of the Mahabharata's twelfth book.

1. Bhishma said, 'On this subject they recite this ancient account of the words spoken by King Vichakhnu as a result of his compassion for all creatures.

2. After seeing the mutilated torso of a bull, the king became aware of the terrible screams of the cows in the animal stockade provided for the sacrificial arena.

3. He then made the following pronouncement, ""May there be good fortune for cows in all parts of the world."' This prayer was spoken when the slaughter of animals began.

4. Such violence is praised only by men who do not adhere to the proper rules. They are fools, unbelievers and doubting souls who always keep themselves concealed.

5. The virtuous Manu has asserted that all ritual acts must be free of violence. It is due to desire and attachment that men afflict animals in the space around the sacrificial altar.

6. A wise man should therefore pursue the subtle science of dharma by performing his duty on the basis of authority. Not harming other beings is certainly recognised as superior to all other forms of dharma.

7. The proper mode of religious life may involve fasting, being resolute in one's vows, and renouncing unacceptable Vedic rules. Selfish persons who seek material gain from such rituals do not follow this path.

8. When men pay close attention to different forms of ritual and to the proper trees to use for the sacrificial posts but then heedlessly feed on the flesh of animals, this is not a form of dharma that is highly regarded.

9. Indulgence in meat, honey, wine, fish, rum and other similar foods has been introduced by dishonest men. Such conduct is not in fact ordained by the Vedas.

10. It is due to desire, delusion and greed that such deviations have been introduced. Brahmanas should
perceive only Vishnu in all their sacrifices and it is ordained that the worship of Vishnu is to be performed
with oblations of milk."'

From the perspective of a historian of Indian religion there
are a number of interesting points to note in this passage,
not least the fact that this condemnation of ritual violence
comes from a source that would usually be regarded as Hindu rather than Buddhist or Jain. It is probably for this reason
that the approach adopted is not to simply deny the validity
of the Vedic revelation, as a Buddhist or Jain commentator
might do, but rather to attempt to reinterpret the tradition
by stating that the killing of animals is not a true part of the
Vedic teachings on ritual practice. This attempt is somewhat
questionable, but again what we can see is the moral principles of compassion and not harming being elevated above
ritual practices as the highest expression of dharma.

The other question Vichakhnu raises here is the motivation of priests and their patrons in causing rituals of this
type to be performed. These practices are not to be regarded
as any expression of piety or devotion to a Deity but are motivated simply out of desire for the material reward believed
to be obtainable through ritual acts. Hence the moral equation that Vichakhnu poses here is whether it is justifiable in
terms of dharma to pursue one's own desires for gain and
pleasure by inflicting suffering on other living beings. Clearly the text here does not accept that view and this broader
context is one that can be applied to the issue of diet, the
eating of meat and even the way in which the dairy industry
produces its goods.

Bhishma continues his words of instruction into Book 13 of the Mahabharata, which is in fact known as the Anu-sasana-parvan, the Book of Instruction. When he turns to the topic of the ritual offerings to be made for the benefit of ancestors in the afterlife, Bhishma again indicates that meat offerings are acceptable and even recommended as most beneficial. At this point, however, Yudhishthira again interrupts the discussion by raising the question of cruelty in the slaughter of animals. He begins with the words *ahimsa paramo dharma ity uktam bahushas tvaya*, 'You have stated many times that not harming (ahimsa) is the highest expression of dharma,' and then questions how offerings of meat can be compatible with this moral perspective. Bhishma entirely accepts what Yudhishthira has said and in response presents a eulogy of vegetarianism. Here is an extract from that speech as it is found in Chapter 116 of Book 13.

20. A learned person who gives the gift of safety to all creatures is regarded as the giver of life to the whole world.

21. This is praised by men as the highest dharma. The life of other creatures is as dear to them as one's own is to oneself.

22. So people who are intelligent and pure-hearted should always act towards other creatures as they would like other creatures to act towards them. Death is a source of fear even for the wise.

23. And how much more so for those whose happiness is found only in this world and who are sought out to be killed by wrongdoers who live by means of killing animals.

24. Therefore, great king, you must understand that giv-

ing up meat is the highest abode of dharma, the highest abode of heaven and the highest abode of happiness.

25. Ahimsa is the highest form of dharma, ahimsa is the greatest act of restraint, ahimsa is the greatest truth. Ahimsa is the basis from which dharma arises.

26. Meat cannot be obtained from grass, wood or stone. It cannot be obtained unless a living being is killed. Hence there is a great fault in the production and consumption of such food.

There are a number of points we could note in this passage but what is particularly interesting is the fact that Bhishma does not make reference to any belief in an afterlife or reincarnation to support his argument for ahimsa. Rather it is the simple moral equation we encountered earlier in relation to animal sacrifice. He points out that for every creature life is the dearest thing and hence to deprive a creature of life is the greatest harm one can do to it. Later on the question arises as to whether or not the eating of meat is essential to sustain our lives and Bhishma accepts that this may perhaps be the case in certain situations. Overwhelmingly, however, the eating of meat is undertaken in pursuit of pleasure and hence the question is posed as to whether it is morally justifiable to pursue a form of pleasure that inflicts the worst type of fear and suffering onto another living being. This is a question we shall return to later when we consider the practical application of the concept of dharma we have explored in these earlier sections.

12

Are Dogs Allowed in Heaven?

*I shall never give up on those who need my help until I have
lived my last breath.*
Yudhisthira

No act of kindness, no matter how small, is ever wasted.
Aesop

In the west the dog has truly become a man's best friend
but other cultures and religious traditions have not looked
so favourably upon them. In ancient India dogs were considered the dirtiest of animals, a factor that makes our final
narrative even more interesting. As we have described on
numerous occasions, Yudhisthira is represented by the Mahabharata as being the *dharma-raja*, the 'king of dharma',
and a reading of the final chapters of the Mahabharata again
shows why he is given this title. Here is an account of the
final journey of the five Pandava brothers along with their
beloved wife Draupadi.

After they had ruled the kingdom for many years, the
Pandavas were advised by Vyasa to give up their royal status and retire to a lonely retreat in the mountains in order
to focus exclusively on spiritual goals. Yudhishthira then
had Arjuna's grandson, Pariksit, installed as the new king of
their realm and asked Yuyutsu, Dhritarashtra's only surviv-
ing son to supervise government affairs. Then after making
offerings on behalf of their fallen relatives and paying their
respects to the sages and holy men, Yudhishthira, Bhima,
Arjuna, Nakula and Sahadeva all set off for the mountains

of the north accompanied only by Draupadi, their beloved wife. The citizens begged them to stay but Yudhishthira was insistent that it was now time for them to look beyond this world. As they departed from the city of Hastinapura, all the men and women of the royal household followed them for a while before allowing them to depart, but not even his own family members could persuade the king to stay and give up his intensions.

The great Pandavas and the famous Draupadi observed a preliminary fast and set out east. They passed through various different lands seeing many rivers and oceans. Yudhisthira was followed by Bhima, Arjuna, the twins and then the beautiful Draupadi. As they had left Hastinapura a dog had attached itself to the party, and even as they journeyed on into ever more remote regions, this creature refused to give up their comapany. At this point Arjuna had still not cast off his divine weapon the Gandiva bow, but as they reached the shore of the ocean the Pandavas beheld the god of fire, Agni himself, who commanded Arjuna to cast his mighty weapon into the water as he had no further need to display his martial prowess. The five brothers agreed that the time had now come for them to give up their previous role as kings and warriors and so with some reluctance the heroic Arjuna gave up his beloved weapon and watched it sink beneath the ocean's waves.

Restraining their senses, the noble Pandava brothers then turned in a northerly direction until the mighty Himalayas came into view. Crossing beyond this mountain range they saw a vast sandy desert and then saw the towering peak of Meru, the highest of all mountains on this earth. As they were traversing these perilous mountain paths, Draupadi tragically slipped and fell. In distress, Bhima addressed King

Yudhisthira saying 'O Great King, Princess Draupadi never committed any sinful act. Please tell us why she has fallen.'

Yudhisthira responded, 'O Bhima, best of men, although we were all equal to her she favoured Arjuna and had great partiality for him. It was by not treating us with equality that Draupadi's conduct was blemished, dear brother.'

Having said this they continued along the mountain path but as they moved on, the wise Sahadeva tragically slipped from the treacherous cliff to the bottom of the mountain. Seeing this happen, Bhima again asked Yudhisthira, 'He was one who had great humility, he used to serve us all, so tell me the reason why this son of Madri, the great Sahadeva, has fallen?' Yudhisthira responded 'Sahadeva's weakness was that he considered himself to be more intelligent than everybody else, this was his flaw.'

Still followed by the stray dog, the brothers then continued on their path but as Nakula looked back to see his fallen twin and Draupadi he also slipped from the lofty peak. After seeing the other heroic twin fall in this way, Bhima once more spoke to Yudhisthira, 'The beautiful Nakula who loved all people with great affection has now fallen. He was filled with righteousness and was surely a perfect human being. He always obeyed your orders and was unrivalled in beauty so tell me why he has fallen from this mountain.' Yudhisthira said, 'Nakula was a righteous person and was indeed extremely intelligent, his flaw was that he thought that there was nobody as beautiful as him and I believe it is for this reason that he has fallen. He regarded himself as superior in beauty and considered no person his equal, Bhima.'

Oppressed by grief and distress after witnessing Nakula and the others fall, Arjuna was now broken-hearted. That foremost of heroes who possessed the strength of Indra was the next to fall. When Arjuna the invincible warrior fell, Bhima spoke again, saying, 'Yudhisthira, I cannot recollect any untruth spoken by the high-souled Arjuna even when he was overtaken by anger. So please tell me why this evil fate has befallen someone so good.' Yudhisthira replied, 'Arjuna said that he would destroy all of our enemies in a single day. He became proud of his heroic deeds and yet could not achieve what he claimed; I believe this is why he has fallen. Arjuna disregarded all other bowmen and saw them as inferiors. One desirous of success should never carry such negative sentiments.'

As the two of them continued along their path, the mighty Bhima was the next to fall. As he tumbled down the precipice, he called out to Yudhisthira 'I was considered so precious to you, why have I fallen? Tell me if you know!' Once more Yudhisthira spoke, saying, 'You used to eat tremendous amounts and always boasted of your strength, but whenever you were eating, Bhima, you never gave a thought to other people's needs. This was your flaw.' Having spoken these words, King Yudhisthira walked on with only a stray dog remaining as his final companion.

At that point Indra, the King of the Heavens, suddenly appeared on Earth causing an incredible sound to reverberate in all directions. He approached the son of Pandu on a chariot and asked him to join him and go to Heaven. Recognising the great Indra, Yudhisthira said, 'I have just witnessed all my family members falling down. They should also be going to heaven. Without my brothers and wife I have no desire for heaven, O Lord of the Gods. Draupadi the delicate princess deserves every comfort and should come with us. You must permit this.'

Indra replied, 'You shall see your brothers in heaven for

they have already attained that celestial abode along with Princess Draupadi! You have no need to worry, O Chief of the Bharatas, for you have the honour of going to Heaven exactly as you are, without losing your body or experiencing death. This is very rarely achieved.'

Yudhisthira then said, 'This stray dog is completely devoted and loyal to me. He should definitely come to heaven with us. My heart is now filled with compassion for him.'

Indra replied, 'You have achieved immortality and a position equal to mine. O king, you will receive prosperity in every direction, the highest success, for all the beauty of heaven is yours. Quit this foolishness, dismiss this stray dog and cast him away! There is no fault in acting in this way.'

Yudhisthira said, 'O Thousand-eyed Indra, your behaviour is always righteous. I think it is extremely difficult for a noble person who is truly righteous to commit an act that is unrighteous. I do not desire any wealth or prosperity if I am required to cast away this living being that is devoted to me.'

Again Indra replied, 'There is no place in heaven for dogs! There are celestial beings who will take away all your accumulated merit if you take this filthy creature there! Make sure you consider the consequences fully before you act, Yudhisthira. Abandon this dog along with its impurity and let us depart from this world. You are not being cruel or committing any wrong.'

Yudhisthira said, 'The wise say that abandoning anyone who is dependent and devoted is infinitely evil; it is as bad as murdering an enlightened saint. Therefore, Indra, it is my firm decision not to abandon this dog today for having done such a deed I could never again be content. This is the vow I always try to follow: never to abandon one who is terrified, never to abandon one who is devoted to me, never to abandon one who seeks my protection, never to abandon those who are destitute, never to abandon those who are suffering, never to abandon one who has come to me for help, never to abandaon those who are unable to protect themselves, and never to abandon those who fear for their lives. I shall never turn away from those who need my help until I have breathed my last breath.'

Indra said, 'But regardless of the gifts you have given, the rituals you have performed, the sacrifices you have offered and the good deeds you have done, all the merit you have gained will be destroyed simply by the glance of this impure animal. All you have to do is abandon this stray dog and you can reach the heavenly regions enjoyed by gods. You recently abandoned your brothers and your wife and have achieved the divine realm by virtue of your righteous conduct, so why are you so concerned over such a trivial matter? You have renounced everything else, why will you not just give up this dog?'

Yudhisthira said, 'It is known throughout all the worlds that it is impossible to be the friend or enemy of one who is dead. When my brothers and the princess fell, I was completely unable to revive them but as long as they were alive I would never have left them. Causing fear to a living being that has sought protection, harming women, stealing that which belongs to others, and injuring a friend; each of these terrible acts is equivalent to abandoning one who is devoted to you.'

On hearing the compassionate words of Yudhisthira the just, the stray dog then suddenly revealed its true identity as the God of Righteousness, Ddharma personified. Well pleased with Yudhisthira's righteous words, dDharma spoke as follows, 'You are truly virtuous, O King of Kings, for you have great intelligence and follow good conduct. You have true compassion for all living beings, Yudhisthira, and I will now speak of another example of your virtue. Once in the past I tested you in the Dwaita forests when your brothers faced imminent death. Faced with this terrible situation, you disregarded your full brothers, Bhima and Arjuna, and worked to revive Nakula so that your stepmother would not be left childless. On this occasion, dear son, you have chosen to be compassionate to a stray dog even though it would mean giving up and endless existence in the heavenly domain! Therefore, O King, even in heaven there is nobody equal to you.'

Then dDharma, Indra and the other divine beings welcomed Yudhisthira onto the chariot and together they proceeded to the heavenly regions. As Yudhisthira the just, the pride of the Kuru race, was leaving the Earth a blazing light shone everywhere. Then the wise Narada, the greatest of teachers who was respected throughout all worlds, said the following words as they were departing from this world, 'Of all of the celestials who reside in heaven with all their great achievements, Yudhisthira is the greatest amongst them. He is now famous throughout the world for the purity of conduct and he has travelled to heaven in his own human body, a blessing no one has achieved before him.'

In this final narrative, we again consider the approach to life of the exemplar of dharma and are presented with a fascinating allegory. Firstly, the fall of the four brothers and their wife provides an insight into some of the negative vices which can beset us in life. The second part of the story then shows us that compassion is the very essence of dharma, and it must be emphasised that in India dogs were considered the filthiest of animals to be shunned by all who pursued a ritualised lifestyle. Yudhisthira here renounces the joys of heaven out of pure compassion for the lowest creature in creation and thereby demonstrates exactly what is really meant by the concept of dharma. Yudhisthira truly 'weeps with all beings'. His unflinching adherence to dharma always came before any worldly ambitions or material pursuits. As he said to Draupadi, 'I act because I must act. Whether it brings fruit or not, I do my duty like any other householder, not for its rewards but through loyalty to dharma.' Constantly throughout the Mahabharata, Yudhisthira is faced with adversity and is reminded of the personal losses he may face, but he is always unflinching in placing virtue above ambition. Bhima, Draupadi and the others often argue with him and question his actions, and sometimes it is hard to disagree with the points they make. They ask why they should live in austere conditions and miss out on the joys of the world; why the king should cover himself in the tatters of dharma and throw away *artha* (wealth) and *kama* (pleasure). At the same time, one cannot help but admire Yudhisthira's virtue, and often it is the selfless individuals of the world who capture our imagination and hearts. His character can be summed up in a verse spoken by him to Dhritarashtra. He says, 'The promises I make, I keep, for remember I choose dharma over my life and over eternity. Neither kingdom nor sons, neither glory nor wealth can even come up to a fraction of the Truth!'

Indian philosophy often notes the distinction between the theory and the practice, the doctrine and its practical implications. In early texts such as the Bhagavad-gita the word *samkhya* is used to refer to the philosophy whilst the practice is designated as *yoga*. Up to now we have been primarily concerned with the ideology of dharma and we hope that the narratives presented here have provided a clear insight into what is meant by dharma. So now let us go on and discuss what really matters, that is, how to apply this theoretical discussion to the actual lives we lead.

13

Human Kindness

In the joy of others lies our own.
Pramukh Swami Maharaj

Tenderness and kindness are not signs of weakness and despair, but manifestations of strength and resolution.
Kahlil Gibran

In the modern world many of us enjoy a level of affluence that enables us to possess all manner of consumer goods, most of which bring us a degree of pleasure but few of which could actually be described as necessities of life. Nonetheless, the ideology of modernity seeks to persuade us that unless we can gain access to the latest batch of pleasure-giving devices our lives are limited and unfulfilled. As a result, we go week after week to various outlets to part with our wealth in order to obtain objects or services that will never be regarded as much more than trivial pursuits. There is nothing particularly wrong with this, for human beings have always sought pleasure in whatever form it is made available, but the real issue arises when we consider that whilst we spend such large amounts on trivial items, vast numbers of our fellow human beings are desperate for a few morsels of food to assuage their hunger or for a medicine that will prevent their child from dying. The horrifying truth is that every day we have a choice to make between committing money for another trivial pursuit or giving that same money away to enable a child to live and a mother not to be parted from the baby she loves. When the issue is presented in these stark terms it is shocking at both a personal and a social level. Another horrifying factor is that economic analysis tends to show that our affluence is directly the result of the poverty endured in other parts of the world; in other words our affluence is the root cause of starvation and infant mortality.

Of course throughout the history of humanity elite groups have always sought to flourish and enjoy a luxurious lifestyle whilst neglecting the abject poverty of others living around them. One might even say that this is just the way of the world or a reflection of human nature, but the counter-argument must be that the 'way of the world' is the way we choose to make it and 'human nature' is simply the choices we make. Again though, horrifying as these divisions between rich and poor might be, there is no point in trying to inflict a sense of guilt on those blessed with affluence. The poor are not more righteous and the affluent are not necessarily wicked; there seems little likelihood of the world being changed overnight into an ethical paradise in which everybody is willing to share with anyone in need. Moreover, alongside the selfishness and greed there is an incredible amount of genuine compassion for those in need and ordinary people do donate considerable sums of money to help others. If we recall the philosophical understanding of dharma as the defining characteristic of any object then we might suggest that it is this compassionate tendency that is the reality of human nature whilst selfishness and greed are no more than a perversion or a loss of humanity.

It is interesting to note that in Indian thought *kama* (literally 'pleasure' or 'desire') is regarded as one of the legitimate goals of human existence. It is not thought of as being inherently sinful unless it becomes the dominant factor in our personality and thereby excludes any tendency towards dharma, which is also regarded as one of the goals of life and one that is more elevated than kama. So no one is expected to suddenly renounce all of their wealth and live a life of poverty in the service of the poor (though some saints such Jalaram Bapa have done just that), but simply to move the balance a little bit away from kama in the sense of satisfying our own desires and towards dharma in the sense of using the wealth we have for the benefit of others. When we look at the state of the world it sometimes seems like a hopeless task, for 'the poor are always with us' but we must be aware that each life is a world in itself and it is possible to do something small that has a profound effect on someone's life.

In his discussion with Arjuna in the Mahabharata, Krishna defined dharma as action that brings benefit to living beings but he left it up to Arjuna to use his own intelligence in implementing this precept. When we consider global economics this dilemma over how to implement high-minded precepts emerges again. We might simply give a part of what we own away but then who is the ideal recipient for such largesse? If we give to anyone who appears poor or in difficulty then we may be doing little more than funding dangerous addictions or passing on resources to criminal elements who are able to exploit charity as a source of income. Moreover there is a danger that when money is simply given away to anyone who claims to need it we create a damaging social environment in which people's sense of initiative or self-worth may be seriously undermined.

As is often the case, the implementation of dharma requires intelligence and creativity but where there is a commitment to the principle the main obstacle has already been overcome. It is a real challenge to work out exactly what we can and should do but if the commitment to dharma is there, these problems can be surmounted through intelligence, honesty and skilful means. Moreover, one must be wary of any line of thought or argument which leads to the conclusion that we should retain our own wealth and leave people to help themselves. Invariably such ideas are based on a specious logic designed to give legitimacy to greed; the type of ideology we noted in the speech of Duryodhana to his father. We will also recall from the story of the golden mongoose the indication that basic acts of kindness far transcend the value of ritual acts, whilst Swami Vivekananda's concept of constructive Vedanta shows how action on behalf of those in need is in fact the true expression of the philosophy of spiritual unity. We may be daunted by the enormity of the problems faced by the world and the extent of the suffering occurring all around us, but we can also see that so much can be done. Ahimsa is not just a passive mood of not harming; it is also the refusal to allow those who are suffering to remain without help. We may see religion in ritual terms or be drawn towards various forms of spirituality, but in all cases the teachings on dharma make it clear that religion and spirituality are truly manifest only in acts of kindness, charity and compassion. Without these, philosophy, religion and spirituality are only so many fashionable words.

14

The Dharmic Diet

When one's food is pure, one's being becomes pure.
Chandogya Upanishad 7.26.2

*Few of us are aware that the act of eating can be a powerful
statement of commitment to our own well-being, and at the
same time the creation of a healthier habitat. Your health,
happiness, and the future of life on earth are rarely so much
in your own hands as when you sit down to eat.*
John Robbins

When we attempt to apply the understanding of dharma
previously delineated to the question of diet and farming
methods, there are a number of crucial questions that immediately come to mind, not least the desirability of adopt-
ing a vegetarian or even a vegan diet. Before we get down to
the specifics of the issue, however, let us remind ourselves of
the core precepts we are seeking to implement. Firstly both
with this book and with Go Dharmic we have tried to avoid
any tendency to lay down a dogmatic set of rules which everyone is morally obliged to follow. As we have seen from
the speeches of Krishna and Yudhishthira, dharma is subtle
and is more a state of enlightened consciousness than a set
of rules. Hence it is accepted that absolutes are impractical
and unhelpful in considering the application of dharmic
precepts to the issues we encounter. We may use our rational faculties to determine that the killing and exploitation of animals is incompatible with the spirit of dharma,
but that may not necessarily mean that a diet which is ab-

solutely vegetarian or vegan is an unbreakable rule. Rather we seek to first establish the ideal and then try to find the practical means by which we can get as close as possible to achieving that absolute state of living. There is no need for a sense of guilt when we fall short of the ideal, and certainly no sense of superiority over those who do not get as close as ourselves to that absolute standard; words of calumny and blame serve no useful purpose and are generally uttered in order to demonstrate our own superiority rather than for any admirable purpose.

The first issue to resolve is whether or not a person needs to eat animal products in order to sustain life and good health. Opinions vary to some extent on this subject, but overall the best evidence suggests that it is certainly possible to live healthily without animal products and in fact it may well be the case that a vegan diet is more conducive to healthy living than one that includes meat and dairy products. If this premise is accepted, then we are faced with a situation where animal slaughter and the suffering inherent in modern farming methods serve no other purpose than the satisfaction of a craving for the sensory enjoyment of a particular type of foodstuff. The question is whether or not it is morally justifiable for a person to inflict pain and death on an animal simply for the purposes of his or her own pleasure—and from the perspective of dharma this is not a difficult question to answer.

What then about dairy products? Traditionally, in India, milk, butter, ghee, cheese and yogurt have formed a large and intrinsic part of the vegetarian diet currently followed by millions of Hindus, Sikhs, Jains and Buddhists. Yet in the modern world there is a lot of evidence to show that intensive methods for the production of milk can be cruel, keeping cows confined in small enclosures and fed on an unnatural diet. Moreover, it is impossible to separate dairy farming from animal slaughter as cows must regularly give birth to calves in order to produce milk and it is often the case that for dairy farming to be economically viable many of these calves must be sold for slaughter. ++Hence when we attempt to apply the ideals of dharma to diet and food production there is a strong argument to suggest that the ideal approach is to try to select food that causes as little harm as possible.

In India, milk has traditionally been produced without any cows being slaughtered as the Hindus' respect for the cow makes slaughter culturally and religiously unacceptable. Moreover, this form of farming was economically sustainable as bulls were used for agricultural work and thereby fulfilled a vitally important function in drawing ploughs and other vehicles. Today, however, the situation has changed dramatically with the widespread mechanisation of Indian agriculture and the use of tractors rather than bulls. It is not clear how these developments will affect animal husbandry but there are already signs that cow slaughter in India is on the increase and there are many Indian farmers, Hindu and non-Hindu alike, who are willing and able to exploit this opportunity for meat production despite the protests of certain Hindu groups. In the West, the links between dairy and meat production are so close that the two industries are virtually indistinguishable. There are a few organic, slaughter-free milk producers such as the Ahimsa Dairy Foundation but these are few and far between, and produce only small quantities of milk. Nonetheless, a willingness to locate organic, slaughter-free sources of milk and dairy products and to pay the higher price for them is certainly admirable and conforms fully to the principles of dharma.

Another essential matter to consider is the use of organic products. In 2009 in the UK an application was put forward for what the media called a 'battery farm' for cows, which would house an unbelievable 8000 cows in one location. (reference?) Battery farming has become common practice in other parts of the western world, but this, we feel, is stretching the boundaries too far. The Go Dharmic campaign 'Go Organic' promotes organic farming as an easy and immediate dharmic step for those who purchase dairy products. Although the ultimate goal is slaughter free organic dairy, by purchasing organic milk we can ensure that certain criteria of animal welfare are met and suffering is thereby reduced. Organic milk producing cows cannot be given antibiotics on a routine basis, they have to be allowed to graze outdoors, their feed is not genetically modified, and they are raised without the use of artificial pesticides and chemicals in their farming. It is very important to note that by purchasing organic we say no to large-scale intensive farming. Up until the 1940's all the dairy produced in the UK was organic, now it is only 5%. (Reference?)If we are to use dairy products and wish to safeguard certain conditions both for the cows and for our own health, the consumption of organic dairy produce is certainly one option to consider.

What is becoming apparent from this discussion is a confirmation of the frequently encountered assertion that dharma and its implementation are subtle matters. On the one hand it may be argued that a vegan diet is best because it has no association with the slaughter of animals, but a counter-argument might be that organic dairy farming provides a more ethical standard of farming and preserves a relationship with cows which has been in existence for thousands of years. Moreover, without dairy farming far fewer cows would exist in the world. This poses another moral dilemma as to whether a relatively comfortable (Comfortable??) life that ends in slaughter is preferable to never existing at all. There are no easy answers to questions of this type and again each individual must employ his or her own sense of honesty and integrity to reach a decision that can be practically implemented.

Some will also argue that eating fish is morally acceptable because most fish live natural lives in the sea or rivers before they are caught for food and hence the cruelty of animal husbandry will generally be avoided. Of course the counter-argument would be that no one needs to eat fish and hence the unpleasant slaughter of these creatures by the fishing industry is a violation of the spirit of dharma. Others will argue that all food production involves the slaughter of a living being as even vegetarian food is produced by the harvesting of plants and there is some evidence to show that plants also suffer in this process. Indeed, plants may possess some degree of consciousness, but as far as we can be aware the level of sentience in plants is much lower than in animals, and as a result the potential for suffering is diminished. Again, we need to be aware that dharma is not about absolutes, but about making the best of any given situation.

Whatever the view one adopts as to the morality of diet and food production, and the practicality of implementing moral precepts in relation to food, the principle must always be to do as much as one possibly can in any given situation. It may be that a vegetarian diet is genuinely impractical, as for example in the mountainous regions of Tibet where arable farming is impossible or amongst the Inuit people of the far north. However, for the majority of us, it is a choice of pleasure rather than necessity and much of the harm caused can be reduced. One may accept that the vegan approach is a good one, but find it impractical to provide a balanced vegan diet for one's family, especially without the nutrition provided by dairy products. If this is the case, then the argument would be that one try to use organic dairy products whenever this is possible so that the level of harm is significantly reduced. The principle will always be that any progress is positive and to be celebrated, whilst inflexible demands for absolute standards can be counter-productive and often prevent us from moving forward in our dharmic standards.

15

The Problem of Violence

*I object to violence because when it appears to do good, the
good is only temporary; the evil it does is permanent.*
Mahatma Gandhi

*Non-violence leads to the highest ethics, which is the goal of
all evolution. Until we stop harming all other living beings,
we are still savages.*
Thomas A. Edison

There are very obvious reasons why it is so frequently asserted that the very essence of dharma can be encapsulated
in the word 'ahimsa'. The literal meaning of the term is 'not
harming' but it is also understood to indicate a policy or
perhaps a mentality of non-violence, an idea emphasised by
Mahatma Gandhi in the modern era. Any study of history or
indeed a glance at the situation in the modern world will re-
veal the horrific sufferings that are the result of human conflict and this in turn lends support to Gandhi's view that in
acts of violence we see the lowest degradation of humanity.
The debate over violence and non-violence is not, however,
confined to issues of war and peace for violence frequently
takes place at a personal level and can, moreover, be enacted
through words and even thoughts as well as through acts of
physical aggression.

Few of us would seek to deny or make light of the horrific consequences of warfare as every conflict is inevitably
accompanied by heart-rending scenes of grief, pain and destruction. In some parts of the world c, Anyone who wit-

nesses the often extreme suffering of innocent victims must feel revulsion for acts of violence and be aware that warfare represents humanity at its lowest ebb. There can be no illusions about the 'glories of war' or wonderful acts of heroism; war is vile and has no redeeming features; it is the very antithesis of dharma.

And yet if we are to propose a doctrine of absolute pacifism, this in turn will be very difficult to sustain. OpponentsWe could rightly cite cases where violence is the only possible way of preventing acts of aggression and of protecting the innocent. What are we to do if we see a violent assault on a weaker person? Surely to take recourse in an ideal of non-violence is just cowardice and a dereliction of duty. At a national level we must also accept that a nation or community subjected to attack from a violent adversary has the right to defend itself and indeed that the leaders of that state have a duty to do so. Hence the debate over the use of violent means is a complex one that cannot properly be resolved through simplistic formulae or by absolutist positions. Again we are in the position of understanding the fundamental precepts but being obliged to carefully employ our rational faculties in order to find the best means of putting them into practice.

Attempts to resolve this tension between the horrors of warfare and the apparent need to employ violent means have led to various attempts to define what is meant by a just war. We might, for example, suggest that recourse to violent action is justifiable only in defence of oneself or others, and that is exactly the position adopted in ancient times by the Emperor Asoka who ruled over most of India. But then we might also argue that war is justified in order to remove tyrants and bring liberty to an oppressed people; again examples can be cited in which the use of violence might be justified. ThenBut at this point again, very real problems arise. Firstly, whilst the awful consequences of violent action are inevitable, the positive outcome we might seek is uncertain. We must also give some credence to Gandhi's assertions that the means will certainly shape the end achieved, and that nothing good can be produced through actions that are inherently evil.

Secondly, countries go to war for reasons of power, hegemony and the acquisition of resources but are able to claim that their aggression is justified by referring to the notion of a just war. In the past, religion was used to give legitimacy to conquest and imperialist domination, and today we see ideals such as freedom and democracy functioning in the same way to provide a veneer of legitimacy for base warmongering. Whilst the doctrine of a just war appears entirely plausible at a theoretical level, such an idea will inevitably be exploited by aggressive nations who will argue that their wars of conquest are motivated by high ideals.

Hence our conclusion must be that whilst we accept the validity of the idea that the use of violence is sometimes legitimate, we need to be aware that high ideals are very rarely the true cause of a war. Therefore opposition to warfare of all types is the proper position to adopt unless and until it can be shown unequivocally that the use of violent means is indeed justified. War is always evil because of the terrible suffering it causes; it will be very rare indeed that a genuine argument can be made for its legitimate use. Those of an Indian background sometimes refer to the Bhagavad-gita as a text that makes the case for the righteous use of violence, but we must be aware that the teachings of the Bhagavad-gita also insist that such a course of action must be accompanied by a state of mind that is completely free of greed and selfish desire. It is easy to see that persons who have achieved such an elevated state of consciousness will equally be free of the violent impulses and aggressive mentality that are the real causes of almost every conflict. Hence it can also be argued that the Bhagavad-gita is a work that promotes the ideal of ahimsa.

This brings us to the real point of the discussion in that this is not so much a debate about policy and practice but rather about the state of consciousness underpinning national culture and the mentality of individuals. Nations resort to violence not because they believe in a doctrine of just war but because their culture is based to some degree on notions of aggression and domination. Likewise, individuals engage in acts of verbal or physical hostility against others as a reflection of their mentality and not because of a particular belief about ideal conduct. Violence is the overt manifestation of a loss of humanity at a communal or individual level; hence all we can do is to look at our own state of mind and endeavour to ensure that as far as possible it is kept free of such aggressive tendencies and displays a benign disposition towards the world around us. The stated ideal is that we should always try to ensure that the thoughts we think, the words we speak, and the actions we perform will be for the good of the wider world and will never inflict harm or cause distress to others. At a national and political level, the way of dharma dictates that we must consistently oppose militarism on the grounds that such action will always cause intense suffering and rarely if ever do any good for the world. We accept the theoretical validity of the idea of a just war but in practical terms it is highly unlikely that the wars we see being fought today will ever reflect that ideal.

16

The World We Live In

Mother Bhumi, may whatever I dig from you grow back
again quickly, and may we not injure you by our labour.
Atharva Veda

Global warming, along with the cutting and burning of
forests and other critical habitats, is causing the loss of living
species at a level comparable to the extinction event that
wiped out the dinosaurs 65 million years ago. That event was
believed to have been caused by a giant asteroid. This time
it is not an asteroid colliding with the Earth and wreaking
havoc: it is us.
Al Gore

One of the major problems we face in the world today is
the degradation of the natural environment, which has been
caused in part by rapid population growth but also by the ris-
ing demand for natural resources to fuel industrial output.
This is certainly a huge problem that humanity as a whole
has to face, but it seems that all too often political leaders
seek to obfuscate and procrastinate, as the consequences of
their actions in this area are not immediate and the solutions are both unpopular and difficult to enforce. Nonetheless, we cannot permanently avoid the consequences of
climate change, food shortages or the destruction of the environment, and hence we must seek to analyse the cause of
the problem, and the solutions that are open to us.

Where environmental issues are addressed, the solutions
proposed seem to fall into two broad categories. Firstly, we

have the practical and scientific response which argues for population control and for alternative forms of energy production that do not have the same devastating impact on the global ecosystem. Secondly, we have a more philosophical approach according to which the problem can be resolved only through a change in the orientation of contemporary culture, a shift from the emphasis on consumerism, which demands the ever increasing exploitation of natural resources. There is much to be said for both these types of response. On the one hand, human beings have shown themselves to be incredibly resourceful in devising new forms of technology whenever a pressing demand arises and finding new sources of energy that can lessen the damage caused to the natural world. Already we have seen the potential of wind farms, solar power and harnessing the natural movements of the oceans, and it is to be hoped that technologies of this type will be steadily refined and improved in the immediate future. From the other side, however, we can see the strength of the argument which urges that however many technological advances are made in terms of energy production, the earth simply does not have the resources available to support the increasing global demand for manufactured goods, fuelled by the ideology of consumerism and the unending quest for economic growth.

Let us now consider these issues from the perspective of dharma, which has been the main focus of our discussions here. As we have noted many times before, dharma does not mean the rigid adherence to a series of pre-ordained codes of conduct but is really about the creative use of human intelligence in order to bring benefit to all living beings, human or otherwise. Dharma is a natural reflection of the spirit of universal compassion and good will to all. dharma

We must be aware that the very existence of many species is now under threat as the environment they depend upon is being constantly encroached upon in the quest for natural resources. Whenever any species, great or small, is lost, then we as human beings are to be held responsible for the damage and degradation we cause. This is not a religious argument related to a creator and his creation, it is simply an observation about the nature of the world we are a part of and the evil effects of damaging that which is our greatest asset.

Moreover, dharma also entails an appreciation of beauty and wonder, for it is frequently argued that the pursuit of dharma is most efficacious when one is able to live in an environment characterised by natural harmony. The conditions we live in affect our state of mind and one should never doubt the positive influence that natural beauty can have upon us individually and socially. Many will feel that the greatest beauty to be found anywhere is in the hills, forests, rivers and seascapes we can still find around us and hence the idea of destroying that beauty just to satisfy our shallow desires is a grossly irresponsible act that will cause incalculable harm to humanity and to the world as a whole. Furthermore, as noted above, the consequences of the environmental crisis may not be fully experienced until several decades into the future, and hence it can be argued that our present actions and lifestyle will cause suffering and hardship for future generations. Again the dharmic perspective must be that one should always seek to avoid any course of action that will be a cause of suffering, for the compassion we seek to develop is for all beings, whether or not their existence is in the present time.

Contemporary culture is shaped substantially by the free

market economy that has become predominant in recent decades and this embodies an underlying assumption that satisfaction, fulfilment and joy are to be derived substantially through the consumption of products. Advertising is one obvious means through which this ideology is thrust on to the public at large but modern culture as a whole also tends to reflect this view, teaching young people to aspire primarily after the status and wealth that allows increasing consumption. The problem is that a reverence for the natural world does not fall into line with the ethos of consumption and may stand in opposition to it, for those who find contentment in an appreciation of natural beauty may feel less need for a constant intake of consumer goods.

From the perspective of dharma, the ideology of consumption is a false one and is based on the notion that human fulfilment is achieved by superficial aspirations. It is a shallow concept aptly reflected in the shallowness of the world it creates, an industrial wasteland that replaces natural beauty. And the beauty of a state of mind where compassion triumphs over greed is reflected in the beauty of the world, which such a state of consciousness will preserve. The faith in consumerism is a false ideology based on deceit and driven by massive expenditure on advertising to perpetuate the lie that consumption brings happiness; it does not, but the economic elite depends for its status on our acceptance of the lie.

We may also be aware of the Vedantic notion that everything in the world is a manifestation of the divine; in the Bhagavad-gita, when Arjuna asks Krishna for a vision of his divine identity what he sees is the world as the body of God. When Arjuna asks Krishna how divinity can be experienced by a person living in this world, the reply is that the awesome splendour of the natural world lifts the human spirit because this world is imbued with divinity and is itself in one sense divine. Hence we can see that reverence for the natural world is not only based on practical morality and on the wish to nurture beauty but perhaps also on a form of spiritual awakening.

From a practical perspective, however, we will be aware that the world is not going to change overnight and individuals may feel powerless to do anything about the situation they find themselves in. So what can we do? The first and most obvious point is that we need to look at our own way of life and try to find ways, even small ways, in which we can live without damaging the natural world. We can try to consume less energy, we can use public transport or walk and cycle instead of using a car, and perhaps we can become a little less enthusiastic about the acquisition of every new gadget that appears. After all, using what you already have is the very best form of recycling. ze It is sometimes argued that the wealth and the strength of the economy depend upon the type of consumerism we have argued against here, but the creative mind can find alternative models of prosperity that embody a nurturing rather than an exploitative attitude towards the natural world. The human imagination is a vast and largely untapped resource; all that is really required is commitment and the will to do things differently.

17

The Life Divine

*Those who understard adharma to be dharma, and dharma
to be adharma are under the spell of illusion and darkness,
and they always strive in the wrong direction.*
Krishna, Bhagavad-gita

*I reject any religious doctrine that does not appeal to reason
and is in conflict with morality.*
Mahatma Gandhi

On a number of occasions we have emphasised the point
that neither the concept of dharma nor the endeavour to
implement the ideals of dharma in life are necessarily religious. Of course the word 'dharma' is derived from Hindu
sources and we have made extensive use of Indian material,
but this should not be taken as any sort of attempt to purvey
specifically Hindu or Buddhist thinking. The ideas and values encapsulated within the term 'dharma' are universal and
cannot be confined within one specific culture or religion.
For some Buddhists, however, dharma (or dhamma) means
the practices by which an individual can reach the state of
nirvana and thereby end the suffering of rebirth, whilst in
some strands of Hinduism dharma means devotional practices associated with the worship of the Supreme Deity.
From our point of view, however, dharma indicates a type
of conduct aimed solely at promoting the wellbeing of the
world, and even where we have referred to Indian textual
sources it has always been with this vision in mind. But what
then is the status of religion? Many people will feel that the

teachings of religion must by definition transcend anything that human beings can arrive at through the use of reason and the application of principles of justice. So where does adherence to a particular religion fit in with the pursuit of dharma?

There is a widely expressed view that in the modern age religious tolerance is an essential reflection of the enlightened values of contemporary societies, but we must be aware that religion can be a pernicious as well as a positive force in the world, and where religion leads to exploitation or hatred of others, there seems little justification for tolerance. That is not to say that religion should in any way be proscribed or have limitations imposed upon it, but it also cannot be made a special case that is above all criticism. Even a passing knowledge of world history is sufficient to know that in the past and the present religion has been used to support iniquitous political aims based on the domination and suppression of others. ,We might be aware of the words of the Bhagavad-gita where it is stated that those whose minds are clouded by darkness will consider adharma to be dharma, or in other words present pernicious ideals as a form of religion (18.32). In other words, not everything presented as religious revelation is righteous in its intent—at times ideas that are highly damaging are paraded as religious truth. On the other hand, however, we will be equally aware that religion has inspired some individuals towards the highest expression of true dharma. It is therefore not possible to say that religion is inherently good or bad; it can be both or neither. It becomes problematic when selfish individuals ruthlessly pursue their own interests but claim legitimacy on the grounds that they are simply following revealed teachings from a higher source.

Since we have mainly focused on Indian sources, an example from Indian culture may serve most effectively to illustrate the point. It is a well-known fact that for centuries Indian society has been structured around a rigid system of social classes referred to as either caste or *jati*. These class designations are typically based on birth alone and have in the past led to social exclusion and indeed the vicious treatment of certain groups designated as *mlecchas* or outcastes. One of the main achievements of modern India is that to some extent caste-based oppression has been reduced, but there is no doubt that abuse and supremacist attitudes are still prevalent amongst a wide section of Indian society. Moreover, in the past certain individuals have presented a religious defence of caste divisions based on scriptural references, the doctrine of karma and rebirth, and ideas of ritual purity in the performance of religious practices. So there may be a situation where condemnation of an iniquitous social practice is rejected on the basis of religious teachings and in that situation the ideal of absolute religious tolerance may be inappropriate.

Of course such issues are not confined to the Hindu tradition; in all the religions of the world we will encounter situations in which religious teachings are cited to support ideas and practices that run counter to the dharmic ideal of justice and universal wellbeing. The dilemma that arises for religiously minded persons is whether to insist on the validity of religious teachings even where these seem to be opposed to a sense of natural justice. The claim often made by religion is that its own doctrines must be given higher status because they originate from a transcendent source, and revelation must take precedence over human reason. What we have seen in our earlier presentation of selected narratives, however, is an alternative perspective whereby inherited teachings focus on core values rather than details of implementation, with the expectation that the intelligence and integrity displayed by adherents will enable them to make decisions based on justice and virtue, without recourse to inherited dogmas. Hence when there appears to be a contradiction between religious tradition and the wellbeing of the world, then justice and morality must always be given precedence. Regarding the caste-based discrimination in India, we have seen how Hindu teachers have made that choice by challenging the validity of traditional practices and insisting instead on the dharmic precept of achieving the greatest benefit for all beings.

We can certainly criticise religion for giving support and legitimacy to an iniquitous form of caste-based social oppression, but at the same time we must recognise that the most vehement opponents of that system are themselves inspired by the same religious tradition to work on behalf of the oppressed. This tension fully reflects the view on the role of religion in relation to dharma. Where religion inspires individuals towards mercy, kindness, and good will, it is to be wholly welcomed, but at the same time there is no valid reason to 'tolerate' iniquitous action simply because the performers claim to be following their faith. It cannot be reasonable to cite personal or shared faith as the sole grounds for claiming legitimacy for certain types of action. At its best religion can bring people towards the highest fulfilment of their humanity, and from a Vedantic perspective this will happen where the inner divine nature triumphs over the mundane. In truth, a religion which inspires a sense of superiority, which demands conversion, which impels its adherents towards selfish acquisition, or which inspires acts of aggression against others is no religion at all.

18

Who's Helping Who?

These rivers, my dear son, flow towards the east, the western towards the west. They go from sea to sea. They become the sea itself. These rivers do not know that they are nothing but the sea.

Uddalaka Aruni, Chandogya Upanishad

A human being is part of a whole, called by us the Universe, a part limited in time and space. He experiences himself, his thoughts and feelings, as something separated from the rest—a kind of optical delusion of his consciousness. This delusion is a kind of prison for us, restricting us to our personal desires and to affection for a few persons nearest us. Our task must be to free ourselves from this prison by widening our circles of compassion to embrace all living creatures and the whole of nature in its beauty.

Albert Einstein

The Mahabharata is full of examples of common compassion and human kindness, and practical humanistic advice: 'Don't treat others in a way you would not like to be treated', 'How can a man who wants to live himself kill another?', 'Wish for others that which you wish for yourself', 'Do not act towards others in a way which is unpleasant and undesirable for ourselves', 'This upright conduct is called dharma and it is determined alone by kindness'.

In this section, however, we would like to discuss the esoteric world view of the Upanishads as an impetus for dharmic action. In this grand vision we are no longer simply providing charity from the privileged to the underprivileged but serving our true self. The Upanishads suggest the notion that the underlying basis of the universe is essentially one existence (*Brahman*), and that the very essence of all living beings, the soul or self, is a part of this whole : 'I am I'; 'I am Brahman'; 'I am all'; 'You are that'.

In the Chandogya Upanishad, Uddalaka Aruni instructs his son Svetaketu, 'These rivers, my dear son, flow towards the east and towards the west. They go from sea to sea. They become the sea itself. These rivers do not know that they are nothing but the sea and similarly, my dear son, all these beings, even though they come forth from one existence, they do not know the reality of that existence. Whatever they are in this world, be it tiger, lion, wolf, bear, boar, fly or mosquito, they are in essence all the same. That which is the finest essence of our being this whole world has for its self. This is the truth of the self; you are that, Svetaketu.'

The early Sanskrit scholar Paul Deussen explained, 'The Gospels quite rightly establish as the highest morality, "Love your neighbour as yourselves". But why should I do so, since by the order of nature I feel pain and pleasure in myself, not in my neighbour?' He goes on to say that in the Vedas, in the three words of the great formula *tat tvam asi*, 'You are that', there is an ideal combination of metaphysics and morality: 'you should love your neighbour as yourselves, because you are your neighbour'.

Another interesting passage is to be found in Chapter Two of the Taittiriya Upanishad, where a teacher gives instruction to his pupil, saying, 'Speak the truth, practise dharma, do not neglect truth, do not neglect dharma, do not neglect study or the welfare of others.' In the next verse, he goes on to explain this instruction to the student:

'Be one who treats his mother like a god. Be one who treats his father like a god. Be one who treats a teacher like a god. Be one for whom the guest is a god. Whatever deeds are without blemish, they are to be practised and not others.' This instruction clearly indicates virtue based not on common decency but on the common identity of beings of this world with the Supreme Reality. Many of the most respected proponents of this ideal were not necessarily great Sanskrit scholars; they simply showered unconditional love and compassion to all they met on the basis of their personal awakening and realisation. Jalaram Bapa, a saint from Virpur, Gujarat, used his temple to feed the hungry and poor, whilst Neem Karoli Baba from North India became famous amongst westerners for his ability not only to love everybody unconditionally but to make others feel as if they also loved everybody. When questioned as to how one could find God, his reply was 'Serve people,' then when asked how one could raise *kundalini* or spiritual energy, he said 'Feed people'.

In the modern world Swami Vivekananda adopted this Upanishadic idea of the common identity of all living beings and used it to support his demands for social reform in India. He called this view 'constructive Vedanta'; here is an excerpt from one of his speeches that illustrates the point:

'I wish that every one of us could come to such a state that even in the vilest of human beings we could see the Real Self within, and instead of condemning them say, "Rise thou effulgent one, rise thou who art always pure, rise thou birthless and deathless, rise almightily, and manifest thy true nature. These little manifestations do not befit you." This is the highest prayer that Vedanta can teach you. This is the one prayer, to remember our true nature, the God who is always within us, thinking of it always as infinite, almighty, ever-good, ever-beneficient, selfless, without any limitation. And because that nature is selfless, it is strong and fearless; for only through selfishness comes fear.'

Whilst campaigning throughout the world for dharmic reform on the basis of this Vedantic outlook he said, 'No dogmas will satisfy the cravings of hunger. These are two curses here, first our weakness, secondly our hatred, our dried-up hearts. You may talk doctrines by the millions, you may have sects by the hundreds of millions; aye, but it is nothing until you have the heart to feel; feel for them as your Veda teaches you, till you find they are parts of your bodies, till you realise that you and they, the poor and rich, the saint and the sinner, are all parts of one infinite whole, which you call Brahman.'

By reading this passage we can easily get a feel for how this vision could be implemented. Mahatma Gandhi employed a similar philosophy in his non-violent resistance against British rule, untouchability, religious discrimination and the mistreatment of Indian women. He wrote, 'I want to realize brotherhood or identity with all life, even such things which crawl upon earth. [. . .] all life in whatever form it appears must be essentially one.' His philosophy based on non-violence, love and compassion drew inspiration from a similar worldview, whereby the self is recognised as being beyond caste, gender, ethnicity, or any other form of distinction that might divide us.

This outlook is not confined to Hindu philosophy. Islamic Sufism, Egyptian Gnosticism and many other spiritual teachings have followed a similar line of thought. Bhai Kanhaiya, a prominent Sikh devotee of Guru Tegh Badhur Singh, became famous for feeding and providing water to injured Moghul adversaries on the battlefield after a war. When he was summoned in front of the Guru and questioned as to why he was undertaking such an apparent act of treachery, his response was 'I see no Mughal or Sikh, only human beings filled with God's spirit. Guruji, have you not taught us to treat all people equally?' The guru was very satisfied and said, 'From now on you should also take medicine with you.'

This approach could inspire the dharmic action that is required in the world. The enlightened ones who have realised the existence of their own self in others will dedicate their whole lives to working for the welfare of the world, but even a slight move away from baser impulses and the pursuit of selfish ends could provide us with a method for reducing the burden on the earth, the animals, and ourselves.

In India and many other parts of the world male-dominated social structures have often forced women to accept an inferior position. Again, however, we can find significant ideas in Indian literature that can provide inspiration and empowerment for women. One excellent exemplar is Sulabha, a strong woman, single by choice, who is described in the Mahabharata as a learned philosopher who triumphs over kings and pundits in philosophical debate, showing that their dismissal of her as a woman is based on ignorance and base sentiments. She successfully overcomes the powerful King Janaka by logically establishing that higher realisation of the true self reveals that there is no essential difference between a man and a woman; she also demonstrates by her own example that a woman may achieve the highest level of spiritual enlightenment. Many religions in the face of modernity face decisions on whether women can be ordained as bishops, imams, priests or swamis, whether they can worship equally with men without discrimination. The Upanishadic notion of absolute equality would of course support Sulabha and others like her, and we think the true understanding of dharma would, too.

Although inequalities based on gender, sexuality and race are all important issues to be addressed, the modern world view is particularly preoccupied with youth. As a result the elderly are sometimes disregarded and can suffer from depression, loneliness and lack of proper care. There have been studies of societies where individuals live longest in the world; Okinawa, Japan is one such example. Although there is no single reason for this, and diet, exercise and other factors all play a role, it is no surprise that those societies with significant numbers of healthy, active centenarians all treat the elderly with dignity, love and respect. As families become less closely bound together and priorities change away from mutual concern towards wealth accumulation, the elders of a family can be seen as a burden rather than wise members of society who have an important role to play. This is another area of concern for those interested in cultivating a more dharmic world, and it is very unfortunate that many young people do not grow up in the company of wise, loving elders.

As Krishna says in the Bhagavad-gita (6.32), *atmopamyena sarvatra samam pasyati*, 'seeing everybody as identical to oneself', summarises the spiritual motivation for this kind of morality.

19

Go Dharmic

Let us come together, talk together, let our minds be in harmony, common be our prayer, common be our end, common be our purpose, common be our deliberations, common be our desires, united be our hearts, united be our intentions, perfect be the union among us.
Rig Veda 10.191.2

Considering the welfare of the world, you ought to act.
Krishna, Bhagavad-gita, 3.21

Things will not change unless we act. As Bhisma aptly instructs Yudhisthira, 'One who renounces all action and resorts to destiny alone is a like a woman who expects children from an infertile husband. Human exertion must follow destiny, but destiny alone cannot create results where human exertion is absent.' His humorous but wise exhortation encourages us to always remain active. It is not acceptable for us to allow our brothers and sisters to suffer and simply excuse our inaction on the basis of its being their bad karma or some other form of specious reasoning. On the contrary, the real bad karma is in the lack of proper action.

Indian teachings show great concern for social stability and the general good of society as a whole. In the Bhagavad-gita, Krishna argues that Arjuna must think of the good of society in his consideration of action: *loka-samgraham evapi sampasyan kartum arhasi*, 'Considering the welfare of the world, you ought to act' (3.21).

Daya Bhuteshu, those who follow the Gita's advice must

take whatever action they can to alleviate the suffering of others. It could be argued that poverty and environmental degradation arise as a direct result of human greed —if, however, nations and individuals could embrace Krishna's assertion of *aloluptva*, the absence of this greed, then this would be a major step towards solving the problems we have considered here.

With this understanding the case becomes clearer. The ideal of dharma we have explored here gives the broad principles, the virtues we must seek to integrate into our lives. It is up to us to sincerely acknowledge these virtues and to vigorously seek to implement them in whatever manner seems most appropriate.

The exemplary role models provided by the narratives draw the mind towards the path of dharma and these accounts must be preserved and promoted so that the ideology of dharma can challenge the materialist tendencies inherent in modernity. From Nachiketas, we need to learn to choose the *sreyas* over the *preyas*. Rama should inspire us to become embodiments of virtue. From Krishna we need to learn to apply our common sense in every situation and from Yudhisthira we need to learn to be compassionate to all living beings. By telling the story of the the golden mongoose we can remind ourselves that feeding the poor is more profoundly spiritual than elaborate rituals or esoteric practices. King Yayati spent a thousand years in pursuit of his pleasures but finally found fulfilment in living a simple, peaceful existence and displaying a mood of love to all. Savitri was steadfast in her commitment to dharma and we have seen this same courage in the lives of Narayan Guru, Mahatma Gandhi, Martin Luther King and Nelson Mandela.

King Yudhisthira said to Indra, the King of the heavens, 'I

do not desire wealth, prosperity, or heaven if I am required to cast away this dog that is now devoted to me.' In a world where suicide bombers take the lives of innocent men, women and children in the hope of achieving heavenly rewards, Yudhisthira's choice to care for the dog is astounding. The timeless truths found in these narratives have changed the lives of millions of people over the centuries and to this day they have the power to provide us with practical inspiration. The more people understand dharma and commit themselves to bringing forth dharmic change, the more chance we have for a better future for our children. Dharmaeir—As we learn from Yudhisthira the satisfaction we can get from dharma is beyond material success and even the highest heavenly rewards.

GO DHARMIC BOOKS

By Hanuman Dass & Dr. Nicholas Sutton

- *The Power of Dharma: The Universal Moral Principle*
- *The Power of the Hanuman Chalisa*

Dr. Nicholas Sutton

- *The Original Yoga Teachings (Coming Soon)*
- *Questioning Zakir Naik*

Hanuman Dass

- *The Ramayana of Love: A Journey through the Ramacharitmanas (Coming Soon)*

JAICO PUBLISHING HOUSE

Elevate Your Life. Transform Your World.

ESTABLISHED IN 1946, Jaico Publishing House is home to world-transforming authors such as Sri Sri Paramahansa Yogananda, Osho, The Dalai Lama, Sri Sri Ravi Shankar, Robin Sharma, Deepak Chopra, Jack Canfield, Eknath Easwaran, Devdutt Pattanaik, Khushwant Singh, John Maxwell, Brian Tracy and Stephen Hawking.

Our late founder Mr. Jaman Shah first established Jaico as a book distribution company. Sensing that independence was around the corner, he aptly named his company Jaico ('Jai' means victory in Hindi). In order to service the significant demand for affordable books in a developing nation, Mr. Shah initiated Jaico's own publications. Jaico was India's first publisher of paperback books in the English language.

While self-help, religion and philosophy, mind/body/spirit, and business titles form the cornerstone of our non-fiction list, we publish an exciting range of travel, current affairs, biography, and popular science books as well. Our renewed focus on popular fiction is evident in our new titles by a host of fresh young talent from India and abroad. Jaico's recently established Translations Division translates selected English content into nine regional languages.

Jaico's Higher Education Division (HED) is recognized for its student-friendly textbooks in Business Management and Engineering which are in use countrywide.

In addition to being a publisher and distributor of its own titles, Jaico is a major national distributor of books of leading international and Indian publishers. With its headquarters in Mumbai, Jaico has branches and sales offices in Ahmedabad, Bangalore, Bhopal, Bhubaneswar, Chennai, Delhi, Hyderabad, Kolkata and Lucknow.

SINCE 1946